SUSAN B. ANTHONY

SOCIAL REFORMER AND FEMINIST

LAURA BASKES LITWIN

Enslow Publishing

101 W. 23rd Street
Suite 240
New York, NY 10011
USA

enslow.com

Published in 2017 by Enslow Publishing, LLC.
101 W. 23rd Street, Suite 240, New York, NY 10011

Copyright © 2017 by Enslow Publishing, LLC.

Library of Congress Cataloging-in-Publication Data

Names: Litwin, Laura Baskes, author.
Title: Susan B. Anthony : social reformer and feminist / Laura Baskes Litwin.
Description: New York, NY : Enslow Publishing, 2017. | Series: Heroes of the women's suffrage
  movement | Includes bibliographical references and index.
Identifiers: LCCN 2016005249 | ISBN 9780766078888 (library bound)
Subjects: LCSH: Anthony, Susan B. (Susan Brownell), 1820-1906—Juvenile literature. | Suffragists—
  United States—Biography—Juvenile literature. | Feminists—United States—Biography—Juvenile
  literature. | Women social reformers—United States—Biography—Juvenile literature. | Women's rights—
  United States—Juvenile literature.
Classification: LCC HQ1413.A55 L57 2016 | DDC 305.42092—dc23
LC record available at http://lccn.loc.gov/2016005249

Printed in the United States of America

To Our Readers: We have done our best to make sure all websites in this book were active and appropriate when we went to press. However, the author and the publisher have no control over and assume no liability for the material available on those websites or on any websites they may link to. Any comments or suggestions can be sent by e-mail to customerservice@enslow.com.

Photo Credits: Cover, p. 19 GraphicaArtis/Archive Photos/Getty Images; cover, interior design elements: wongwean/Shutterstock.com (grunge background on introduction, back cover); Attitude/Shutterstock.com (purple background); Sarunyu_foto/Shutterstock.com (white paper roll); Dragana Jokmanovic/Shutterstock.com (gold background); Eky Studio/Shutterstock.com (grunge background with stripe pattern); macknimal/Shutterstock.com (water color like cloud); Borders-Kmannn/Shutterstock.com (vintage decorative ornament); p. 5 Everett Historical/Shutterstock.com; p. 9 Lee Snider Photo Images/Shutterstock.com; p. 11 Museum of Fine Arts Boston, Massachusetts, USA/Bequest of Maxim Karolik/Bridgeman Images; pp. 14–15, 72 © North Wind Picture Archives; pp. 23, 30, 35, 48, 64, 65, 77, 81, 93, 97, 99, 106, 111 Library of Congress, Prints and Photographs Division; p. 27 Joseph Kyle/File-Mott Lucretia Painting Kyle 1841/Wikimedia Commons; p. 33 SSPL/Getty Images; p. 39 Fotosearch/Archive Photos/Getty Images; p. 42 Kean Collection/Archive Photos/Getty Images; p. 51 Carl Simon/Bridgeman Images; p. 56 Elizabeth Cady Stanton and Susan B. Anthony/File:Womans National Loyal League 1863 Call/Wikimedia Commons; p. 61 National Archives; p. 69 Hulton Archive/Getty Images; p. 84 National Woman Suffrage Association/First pg-File:Declaration of Rights Women1876-I/Wikimedia Commons; p. 87 Universal History Archive/UIG/Getty images; p. 104 Cincinnati Museum Center/Archive Photos/Getty Images, p. 112 Hinda Mandell.

CONTENTS

RESTRICTED

For a very long time in America, men made all the laws. For almost a century and a half from the time our country was founded in 1776, they made laws that gave them control over women's lives. Before 1920, to be female in the United States meant to have no rights.

When girls were educated at all, their studies were stopped years earlier than boys. Most high schools and colleges refused to admit girls. If a young woman was lucky enough to avoid domestic service or a factory job, she was overwhelmingly likely to be home learning how to cook and sew.

Once a woman married, the law literally said she belonged to her husband. Any money she earned was his. Any property they had he owned. By law, even their children were his alone.

Before 1920, a woman's life was so restricted that merely speaking in public, particularly before an audience that included men, was considered outrageous and indecent. Women who dared try to speak were routinely shouted down and intimidated.

Women were confined by their clothes. A typical dress and petticoat had so many layers of

Susan B. Anthony (1820-1906) was a founder of the women's rights movement in the United States. Her decades-long fight ultimately resulted in women's suffrage.

material it weighed over 10 pounds (4.5 kilograms). Tight corsets made from whale bones crushed small ribs. Long skirts dragged in puddles and often caused women to trip and fall.

At church, wives listened to sermons with bible passages reminding them to submit to their husbands as well as their God. At home, the responsibilities of child-rearing were unquestionably all the mother's.

Before 1920, American culture was shaped by the idea that women were by naturally more suited for the home. A true woman was defined as a dutiful wife and a loving mother. She was meant to stay at home and if she did venture out, a man had better be by her side.

In 1920, everything changed. On August 18, the Nineteenth Amendment to the Constitution was ratified, giving women the right to vote. Winning the right to vote was the essential first step to changing the unequal laws and customs that had been in place in the United States for nearly 150 years.

The woman who led the charge for getting women the vote —or suffrage, as it is called — could not be there to celebrate its victory. Susan B. Anthony had died fourteen years earlier. Yet it is safe to say that the jubilant crowds that summer day were loudly cheering her name.

For over fifty years Susan B. Anthony devoted her life to the cause of women's suffrage. Born into a world entirely ruled by men, Anthony boldly envisioned a society where women could enjoy all the same rights.

Though she never married, she fought for the rights of wives to keep their wages and own property. Though she never had the opportunity to go to college, she fought for young women to attend. Though she never had children, she fought for the right of mothers to have shared legal guardianship.

Rejecting the notion that women remain silent in public, Anthony gave thousands of speeches across the country. She was screamed at, pelted with eggs, and her life was threatened. Still, she became one of the most popular lecturers in America.

In fact, she was one of the most famous people in the country. Her birthday was proposed as a national holiday. Just before she died, President Theodore Roosevelt sent her a handwritten birthday card. For many eighty-six year-olds, this would have been an exciting milestone.

For Susan B. Anthony, wishes from the president were not enough. She told her friend, "I would rather have President Roosevelt say one word to Congress in favor of amending the Constitution to give women the suffrage than to praise me endlessly."[1]

Anthony's response was a typical one for her. Never afraid to speak her mind, this most unconventional woman did more than perhaps any other in her time to help change women's lives for the better. America can claim her as one of its greatest patriots.

CHAPTER ONE

EARLY LIFE

Susan Brownell Anthony was born on February 15, 1820, in her family's farmhouse in the small rural town of Adams, Massachusetts. In 1820 America was formed by just twenty-three states, bordered in the west by the Mississippi River. That same year James Monroe won his second term as the country's fifth president.

Adams, Massachusetts, was in a beautiful part of the young United States. Small farms dotted a rolling green valley. The Hoosic River ran through the center of town and the Berkshire Mountains rose high in the distance. The community in which Susan was born was a close-knit one.

Susan's father, Daniel Anthony, was a Quaker, a member of a religious group also known as the Society of Friends. The group got this name because above all else they valued friendship. Quakers believed every person was equal before God and deserving of the same fairness and respect.

Quaker worship was different from that practiced in other churches. In their services, people prayed silently, speaking aloud only when they wanted to include someone else in their prayers. No minister was considered necessary because Quakers believed that God's spirit was already inside every soul. They called this a person's inner light.

Reaching the inner light took serious work. Quakers wore plain clothes and spoke formally, using "thou" and "thy" instead of you and I. No toys or games or even music were allowed in the Anthony house. While Susan and her siblings might not have known any different, their mother, Lucy, most certainly did.

Lucy Read had been raised a Baptist. Baptists went to church every Sunday but also believed it was fine to wear bright clothing or sing and go to parties. Lucy gave this all up to marry Daniel, though a few nights before her wedding, she stayed out dancing until four in the morning for a final party.[1]

While Lucy quit her freer ways, Daniel defied his church. The Quaker elders were not pleased by the marriage of one of their own to an outsider. They demanded that Daniel make an official apology in front of

Susan B. Anthony was born in this farmhouse in Adams, Massachusetts, in 1820. When Susan was six years old the Anthonys moved to New York State.

the congregation. Lucy decided not to become a Quaker herself but adopted many of their simple ways, dressing in gray and raising her eight children as Friends.

THE IMPORTANCE OF EDUCATION

Quakers allowed women to be church elders and encouraged the same education for girls as boys. Susan learned to read by the time she was four and went to the same public school as her brothers. One day she came home angry because her male teacher refused to show her how to do long division just because she was a girl.[2] Daniel Anthony set up a new school for his children at once, teaching them himself at first and then hiring teachers.

In business, Daniel Anthony was also moving forward. The brand new invention of the power loom allowed the mass production of cotton cloth. America had entered the Industrial Age. Hardworking and ambitious, Anthony was anxious to take advantage of new opportunities.

The textile mill he ran became so successful that he moved the family one hundred miles (160 kilometers) away to Battenville, New York, where he was hired to supervise the operation of several mills. Daniel employed many people in town and made frequent trips to New York City to sell the goods he produced.

The Anthony family moved into a new brick home. The house had fifteen rooms and four fireplaces but was decorated in the plain Quaker tradition. Many windows brought in natural light. Inside, the plaster walls were painted white, and the furniture was simple and functional.

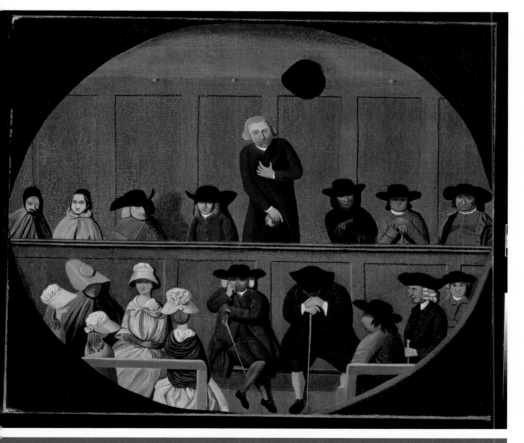

This oil painting depicts a Quaker meeting. The Anthony children were raised as Quakers like their father, Daniel, and were exposed to the social reform advocated by many Quaker groups.

If they were off from school, the Anthony children were expected to work at the mills. When Susan was eleven, she earned $3 for two weeks labor at the loom and used the money to buy her mother some blue teacups. At the same time, she suggested to her father that he promote a young woman she thought would make a good supervisor. Her father said he would not consider any woman for the position, a refusal that confused and disappointed Susan.[3]

Throughout her youth, Susan would be among girls who earned their own living. Many worked at the mill and groups of them took their room and board at the Anthony home. Susan helped her mother prepare meals and clean rooms for as many as two dozen people.

In the fall when she was seventeen years old, Susan joined her older sister at Deborah Moulson's Female Seminary, a Quaker boarding school outside of Philadelphia. The school taught girls a curriculum as rigorous as any boys' school. Susan studied biology, philosophy and literature.

The headmistress was very strict and Susan often bore the brunt of her anger. In a diary she kept at the time, she described how her teacher made her feel like a "vile sinner" simply because she did not dot an "i" in her composition book.[4]

In part because her teacher was so hard on her, but also because the childhood she had known

MATILDA JOSLYN GAGE 1826–1938

Matilda Joslyn Gage was a longtime antislavery supporter and raised in a home that was a destination on the Underground Railroad. One of the most gifted writers in the women's movement, she worked with Susan B. Anthony and Elizabeth Cady Stanton on *The Revolution,* the first three volumes of the *History of Woman Suffrage,* and the Philadelphia Centennial "Declaration of Rights for Women." Matilda Joslyn Gage also was an activist for Native American rights and was made an honorary member of the Wolf clan of the Mohawk tribe.

was a happy one, Susan was exceptionally homesick. A typical letter home included the sentiment, "300 miles [482 km] from the beloved spot, separated from all that is dear to me."[5]

HARD TIMES

Her homesickness would be short-lived, only to be replaced with a different misery. After just one semester, Daniel Anthony's business went bankrupt. Not only could he no longer afford his

Susan operated a loom at her father's textile mill when she wasn't in school. Single women were permitted to work and earn money. They actually had greater rights than married women during this time.

daughters' tuition, he lost everything else. The mills and the family's home had to be sold. All their possessions were put up for public sale.

The long list of personal items to be auctioned went far beyond the furniture. It covered all the food in their pantry and all their books, including the family bible. Even their underwear and eye-glasses became part of the sale inventory.[6]

Daniel Anthony was not the only business-man to lose everything that year. The Panic of 1837, as it would become known, caused an economic depression across the country that would last another five years. Many people lost their jobs and life's savings.

At the last minute, the family avoided the embarrassment and grief of having to sell their belongings when Joshua Read, Lucy Anthony's brother, agreed to buy them back instead. Daniel promised to repay his brother-in-law as soon as he was able.

The Anthony family moved to a nearby town called Hardscrabble, a name that seemed to echo their new tough circumstances. Daniel found a house where the family would be able to live and take in borders to cover their rent.

Susan's older sister Guelma, with whom Susan had been at school, soon announced she was getting married. Guelma had known her fiancé since she was a girl, but it is likely the couple decided to step up their plans to marry in light of the Anthony's financial problems.

Susan took the news hard. Guelma was her closest friend and Susan could not resign herself to losing her sister to a separate life. Still, she recognized that most young women of her time were choosing to marry. If a woman did not have a husband she would need to figure out a way to support herself.

For Susan, the choice was self-reliance. As a Quaker she had been raised to value this. Perhaps more important, by nature she was independent and strong-willed. She saw that her life was about to change in a big way. She asked to be called Susan B., abbreviating her middle name for the first time.

Susan B. Anthony understood her formal education was officially over. She would now need to earn money to support herself and help her father pay down his debts. She was only nineteen years old, but the responsibilities of adulthood were fully upon her.

CHAPTER TWO

THE STUDENT BECOMES THE TEACHER

Susan B. Anthony took a job as a teacher at a small Quaker boarding school in New Rochelle, New York, a town about 25 miles (40 km) outside of New York City. The school was run by a woman named Eunice Kenyon. Eunice Kenyon was a completely different sort of headmistress than Deborah Moulson, the overly strict teacher at the school Susan had attended.

Eunice Kenyon was kind and open to new ideas. Even though it was Susan's first job, Eunice encouraged her to experiment with various teaching methods and decide which worked best for her in the classroom.[1] While she could not pay Susan much of a salary — only $10 a week — her school was a good place to work.

Perhaps because Susan had gone to a school where harsh discipline was the rule, she was a stern teacher herself. Maybe she felt she needed to be tough because she was young and the age difference between her and the older students was a

Throughout her twenties and thirties, Susan B. Anthony focused on the profession of teaching. She actively chose not to marry for the sake of being married, and remained single throughout her life. This allowed her to devote more of her time to the cause of women's rights.

small one. Whatever the reasons, the children were afraid of their Miss Anthony.

One student's mother even came to the school to complain. In another setting, Susan might have been fired for circumstances like this. Eunice Kenyon not only backed her new teacher, she publicly stated her support.[2] With her first job, Susan B. Anthony was very fortunate. She was encouraged to be independent, and she was given real responsibility.

Teaching was one of the few professions open to educated women in this era. As instructors, tutors, and governesses, women were looked upon favorably as motherly presences, though only a small minority of them were actually mothers. Most important, teaching allowed single women to gain real economic independence.

Yet while Susan's situation was in many ways a good one, she was exceedingly homesick again. Before the next semester began, she decided to quit her job and return home. The first week that she was back her sister Guelma got married.

In her teens and throughout her twenties and thirties, Susan was courted by a number of men. More than one of these suitors asked her to marry him. One man's proposal included the demand that she stop teaching. Another, an older widower, wanted her to help him run his large dairy farm.

Though she lived in a time when it was expected for a woman to marry, Susan B. Anthony chose to remain single. She would be asked about this decision over and over again throughout her life. Worse, there would be those who attacked her for it.

Perhaps if she had met someone she loved and considered her equal, she might have married. Nevertheless, she never seemed to regret staying single. She once told a newspaper reporter, "I never said I would not marry. Simply this, I never found the man who was necessary to my happiness. I was very well as I was."[3]

For the next decade, Susan continued to work as a teacher. She began at a public school near her family's home and then became a governess. By 1845, Daniel Anthony's financial situation had recovered enough that he was able to purchase a farm just outside of Rochester, New York.

Susan helped her family settle into their new home, but moved herself nearly 200 miles (321 km) away to accept a position running the girls' school at Canajoharie Academy, a private high school. There she was in charge of twenty students. As headmistress, she taught the girls English, math, botany, philosophy, and history.

At Canajoharie, Anthony was paid a salary of $110 for the year. While this was not much, it was the most she had ever earned.[4] Since her father was now making some money again himself, for the first time she was able to keep her whole paycheck. Susan bought a new hat, a new shawl, and some dresses. Her new clothes were brightly colored—in plaids and with fringes—very different from the plain Quaker attire she had worn her whole life.

She stopped using the more formal Quaker speech. She even went to a dance, something Quakers never permitted themselves. When her date had an alcoholic drink however, she drew the line, saying, "I cannot think of going to a dance with one whose highest delight is to make a fool of himself."[5]

For once, homesickness did not overtake her, and Susan found herself growing into a self-confident and strong young woman. Teaching was beginning to seem less challenging to her. She wanted to do something even more important with her life. In a letter to her mother, Susan wrote, "I am tired of theory. I want to hear how we must act to have a happier and more glorious world."[6]

THE TEMPERANCE MOVEMENT

Susan B. Anthony joined the local chapter of the Daughters of Temperance. The temperance movement was against drinking alcohol, a belief shared by the Quaker tradition. Daniel Anthony had been involved with the movement for many years.

Terrible poverty and miserable living conditions, particularly in the new cities that sprang up as the country industrialized, aggravated many existing

Temperance societies sought to banish alcohol. This temperance banner depicts a man being caught between two women: one in white, symbolizing virtue, and another tempting him with alcohol, cards, and dice.

problems. Drunkenness was one of these, with women and children often getting the worst treatment at the hands of alcoholic husbands and fathers.

Susan B. Anthony gave her first public speech at a dinner sponsored by the Canajoharie Daughters of Temperance. Despite the common restrictions on women speaking in public, hers was no timid practice talk. More than two hundred people filled the auditorium and heard Anthony call Canajoharie "a hot bed of vice and drunkenness."[7]

The speech was a rousing success. Susan was able to tell her parents that she had heard "Miss Anthony was the smartest woman now or ever in Canajoharie."[8] Social reform became Susan B. Anthony's new passion. She resigned from her teaching job three weeks later.

SENECA FALLS AND WOMEN'S RIGHTS

On the other side of New York State, in a small town called Seneca Falls, an event had recently taken place to which Anthony had paid little attention. Her parents and youngest sister had attended it without her. Yet it would come to pass that the consequences of this event would completely change the path of her life.

In Seneca Falls, five women had decided to hold a public meeting unlike any other before. Four of the women were Quakers, including Lucretia Mott, a world famous abolitionist, or person who fought against slavery. The fifth woman was Elizabeth Cady Stanton. Stanton was also an ardent abolitionist but she would soon be much better known for her work elsewhere.

The women put an announcement in the local newspaper, the *Seneca County Courier*, that read:

> WOMAN'S RIGHTS CONVENTION — A convention to discuss the social, civil and religious condition and rights of Woman will be held in the Wesleyan Chapel, at Seneca Falls, N.Y., on Wednesday and Thursday, the 19th and 20th of July current, commencing at 10 o'clock a.m.

The call was picked up by other newspapers, as well. The notice had been placed just one week prior to the meeting's planned date and the women were not at all certain anyone would show up. They were also unsure what exactly they should plan for the meeting's agenda.

What moved the women to act was their absolute conviction that the circumstances of women in the United States needed to be improved. The law at this time was brutally clear and harshly unfair. It read simply, "The husband and wife are one, and that one is the husband."[9] What this meant was that a married woman had no legal rights. She could not keep any money she earned, she could not own property, and she could not sign a legal contract. She was not even allowed to be the legal guardian of her children.

Elizabeth Cady Stanton decided to draft a statement of rights for women using the Declaration of Independence as a model. She would call this document the Declaration of Sentiments. Fine-tuning Thomas Jefferson's words she wrote, "We hold these truths to be self-evident, that all men *and women* are created equal."

She followed this with a specific list of rights she believed all women were entitled to. The ninth right on the list was the right to vote. Nowhere in the world did women have the right to vote at that time. This was a very bold demand. It was so bold that Lucretia Mott was afraid that it was a mistake to include. Stanton's husband decided not even to attend the convention after failing to persuade his wife to drop it.

Fortunately many other people decided to come to the meeting. In fact, hundreds of other people came. Elizabeth Cady Stanton gave the first speech of her life and it was an eloquent one. When she got to the part about giving women the vote, Frederick Douglass, the former slave who had become an abolitionist leader, spoke up forcefully in support.[10]

The women at the Seneca Falls Convention agreed that the rights of women in America needed to be improved. However, they differed in their demands. Lucretia Mott, for instance, believed that asking for the vote was risky.

The Declaration of Sentiments was adopted and signed by a majority of the convention's participants. The struggle for women's rights had officially begun, and Susan B. Anthony was not there to witness its first moments of success.

Nobody ever helps me into carriages or over puddles, or gives me the best place — and ain't I a woman? Look at my arm! I have ploughed and planted and gathered into barns, and no man could head me — and ain't I a woman?

SOJOURNER TRUTH (1797–1883)

Sojourner Truth's given name was Isabella. She was a slave until she was thirty years old and she escaped to the home of abolitionists who bought her freedom. She changed her name when she believed she heard God urging her to speak the truth. Though she never learned to read or write, Sojourner Truth's speech "Ain't I a Woman" includes some of the most important words ever spoken in the name of women's rights.

ABOLITIONIST

Having resigned from her teaching post, Anthony returned to her parents' home in Rochester. They had suggested she run the family farm while she decided what to do next with her life. Daniel Anthony had begun working with an insurance company and needed the help.

Susan worked long hours tending to the flower gardens and fruit orchards that the Anthonys owned. At the same time she joined the Rochester chapter of the Daughters of Temperance and continued the work she had begun in Canajoharie.

Soon she became involved with the fight against slavery as well. The federal government had just passed the Fugitive Slave Act, which required by law that any escaped slave be returned to his or her imprisonment. Like many Quakers, Daniel Anthony was a longtime abolitionist. Now he and his daughter worked together.

On Sundays, the Anthony home became an important meeting place for the anti-slavery effort. Many of the most well-known abolitionist leaders of the day gathered there regularly, including Frederick Douglass, William Lloyd Garrison, and Wendell Phillips.

Susan and her father even helped runaway slaves escape on the Underground Railroad. Her diary entry one day read, "Superintended the

LC-USZ62-7816

Harriet Tubman (1823-1913)
nurse, spy and scout

Harriet Tubman escaped from a lifetime of slavery and devoted the next years of her life to helping other enslaved people do the same. In about thirteen trips, Tubman aided in the rescue of seventy slaves.

plowing of the orchard. The last load of hay is in the barn; all in capital order. Fitted out a fugitive slave for Canada with the help of Harriet Tubman."[11]

By the end of 1850, the causes of temperance and abolition had grown to a place of equal importance for Susan B. Anthony. She went to many meetings, organized rallies, and spoke out regularly against the evils of alcoholism and slavery.

Six months later she would attend an antislavery convention in the newly-famous town of Seneca Falls and find the reform movement she would champion like no other.

CHAPTER THREE

IMPORTANT PARTNERSHIPS

During the meetings of the abolition convention Susan B. Anthony was invited to stay at the home of her friend, a woman named Amelia Bloomer. Bloomer was the publisher of a newspaper called the *Lily*, which advocated for temperance reform.

Amelia Bloomer had become famous for being the first woman to wear pants in public, or what quickly became known as "bloomers." Bloomers were different from the pants women wear today. They were loose-fitting trousers that gathered at the ankle. Women wore them under mid-length skirts or long tunic tops.

While bloomers were a very modest form of dress, they still managed to cause a major public outcry. Not many women ever wore them. In fact, it was only a small group of Amelia Bloomer's friends in the temperance and abolition movements who were brave enough to take on women's dress as another cause for social reform.

At this time the clothing worn by women was extremely confining, very heavy, and even unhealthy.

The average dress was sewn with more than 10 pounds (4.5 kg) of material. The corsets worn underneath were made from hard bone. Pulled tightly as they were, the undergarments strained stomach muscles and compressed vital organs. Fashion-conscious women routinely wore gloves and shoes a size too small and balanced 5 pound (2.3 kg) wigs on their heads.[1]

Long skirts further restricted movement. They dragged in the mud and rain puddles. They swept dirt into the home. They made climbing stairs and getting in and out of stagecoaches difficult and dangerous. Bloomers solved many of these issues, but wearing them created new problems.

This cartoon satirizes the popular fad of wearing bloomers by showing role reversal taken to extreme lengths for the time. Men were extremely threatened by the the idea of women dressing in pants and asking for greater rights.

Amelia Bloomer addressed her frequent criticism in the *Lily*, arguing that wearing bloomers was not "going to make us any less womanly or any the more masculine and immodest."[2] But nineteenth-century America was not ready to accept women in pants. Bloomer wearers were hissed at and skirts prevailed.[3]

ELIZABETH CADY STANTON

Susan B. Anthony would boldly wear bloomers for many months before deciding the societal pressures against them were distracting from the other reforms she was fighting for. But Amelia Bloomer's friendship would prove crucial to Anthony for another reason. It was Bloomer who introduced Anthony to Elizabeth Cady Stanton.

Susan had hoped to meet Elizabeth since the Seneca Falls Woman's Rights Convention three years earlier. For Elizabeth, the introduction was equally significant. She would later recount:

> There she stood, with her good earnest face, and genial smile, dressed in gray delaine, hat and all the same color relieved with pale-blue ribbons, the perfection of neatness and sobriety. I liked her thoroughly from the beginning.[4]

While they came from different backgrounds and lived under completely different circumstances,

Elizabeth Cady Stanton and Susan B. Anthony formed a friendship that would survive triumphs and low points. Their partnership was crucial to the success of the women's suffrage movement.

the two women formed a fast friendship and political partnership like few others.

Elizabeth was the eighth of eleven children born to the wealthy Cady clan. Her father was a judge and her mother was from one of the oldest and most influential families in New York State. Elizabeth grew up in a large house with servants and excelled at Johnstown Academy, the only girl in advanced math and language classes.

Yet following graduation when her male classmates left for college, Elizabeth was denied the same option. No college in America would accept a female student. She went instead to the first school in the country established for women's higher education, the Troy Female Seminary. Troy was founded by Emma Willard, a pioneer in women's education.

Growing up, Elizabeth was disappointed time after time by the little her father could do under the law to assist his female clients. As a young child, she once even tried to use scissors to cut from his law books those statutes that she felt were particularly unfair to women.[5]

At twenty-five, she married Henry Stanton, a well-known abolitionist. For their honeymoon they sailed to London to attend an international anti-slavery convention. There Stanton and her fellow female abolitionists, including Lucretia Mott, were forced to sit in a separate room behind a curtain. It was then that Mott and Stanton first began talking about their idea for a women's rights convention.

On the May day in 1851 that she met Susan B. Anthony, Stanton had recently given birth to her fourth child, a fourth son. She would have three more children, including two daughters, before she was through. Family responsibilities would keep Elizabeth Cady Stanton at home for many years.

Susan B. Anthony had few domestic obligations and was eager to start her career in social reform. When a few weeks after their introduction Stanton invited Anthony to come and stay at her home to discuss working together, Susan B. Anthony quickly accepted.

LISTEN, DON'T SPEAK

As much as they led different lives, they also had opposite—but complementary—talents. Writing came easily to Elizabeth Cady Stanton. Alone in her study she drafted stirring speeches but saw few ways to get her words to the outside world. At delivering the message, Susan B. Anthony would have no peer. Susan B. Anthony and Elizabeth Cady Stanton were ideal allies.

The women decided to focus their efforts first on temperance reform. Anthony was chosen to attend the New York State convention of the Sons of Temperance as a delegate of the women's division. Before the event she gathered petitions calling upon the state legislature to ban the production and sale of alcohol.

Yet when she tried to address the convention its chairman ordered her to remain silent. "The sisters were not invited to speak," he said, "but to listen and learn."[6] Susan B. Anthony walked out of that meeting hall and immediately began making plans to start a new temperance organization in which women ran things. She asked Elizabeth Cady Stanton to serve as its first president.

Just three months later, more than five hundred women came together for the first convention of the new Women's New York State Temperance Society. That so many women showed up was thanks to Susan B. Anthony's strong organizing skills. She placed the newspaper notices, found the speakers, booked the hall, and wrote many personal letters urging attendance.

In the fall of 1852, a few months after the successful temperance meeting, Susan B. Anthony attended her first women's rights convention. This was the third national meeting since the first one in Seneca Falls. Elizabeth Cady Stanton was pregnant with her fifth child and could not attend. She asked Anthony to read a letter from her to the audience.

Anthony listened to speeches by Lucy Stone, Lucretia Mott, Antoinette Brown, and Ernestine Rose, the leaders of the new women's movement. Then Susan came forward to join the others on the speakers' platform and read Elizabeth's letter calling for colleges to accept women.

Having delivered Elizabeth's message, Susan daringly offered up one of her own. She stated her

Unlike most women of the time, Lucy Stone attended college. But she became frustrated with the limitations for women, most notably the notion that women should not be permitted to speak in public.

objection to a woman who had been nominated for the group's presidency. The candidate was wearing a sleeveless low-necked dress. Anthony argued that "the earnest, solid hardworking women of this country" could not be represented by this fashion.[7]

Anthony convinced the convention delegates. In modest gray Quaker attire, Lucretia Mott was elected president. Susan B. Anthony was not finished yet. She suggested Mott urge speakers to talk loudly and clearly. "It is an imposition on an audience to have to sit quietly through a long speech of which they can not hear a word," she said. "We do not stand up here to be seen, but to be heard."[8]

BELVA LOCKWOOD 1830–1917

Belva Lockwood married and had a daughter when she was just a teenager and was widowed at twenty-two. To support her family, Lockwood went to college and became a teacher. Support for women's rights led her to attend law school. Belva Lockwood became the first female attorney to argue before the U.S. Supreme Court. In the 1880s, she ran twice for president as the candidate for the Equal Rights Party. In 1906, she won an unprecedented $5 million award for the Cherokee Nation in a territory dispute with the federal government.

A PURSE OF ONE'S OWN

By the conference's end, Susan B. Anthony was thoroughly behind the cause of women's rights and the cause was thoroughly behind her. She was appointed secretary of the national convention. While temperance was still an important issue for her, she began to view it through a new filter.

Anthony had always considered the plight of women married to alcoholic husbands. Yet when she learned that nearly every local temperance society she had helped set up over the previous year had already disbanded, she was faced with a new understanding. With no right to hold money of their own, female temperance advocates could not sustain their organizations.

Of course for women the issue was much greater than merely not being able to print flyers or rent meeting halls. As Susan wrote in her diary, "Women must have a *purse* of their own…there is no true freedom for women without the possession of all of her property rights."[9]

Anthony went to work. She devised a campaign to circulate petitions addressing the property issue. Her strategy was one that is used regularly in politics today but was stunningly innovative for its time. She appointed sixty women — one in each county in New York— to act as captains in their area. The captains would be responsible for gathering signatures.

These captains had to be tough. For one, they had to travel to gather their signatures. Women traveling alone in this era often had to deal with prejudice and hostility. Some innkeepers would not even serve a meal or rent a room to a solitary

Like her sister-in-law Lucy Stone, Antoinette Brown Blackwell graduated from Oberlin College. Although she was denied ordination at first, Blackwell became the first ordained woman minister in the US.

woman. The second big obstacle the captains faced was the very reason for their task-at-hand— they had no money of their own.

Still, in ten weeks they collected six thousand signatures. Elizabeth Cady Stanton took the petitions and went before a joint judiciary committee of both legislative houses in New York State, the first woman ever to do so. Stanton had been reluctant to leave home since her baby daughter was just five months old. Anthony convinced her to go. In a letter to Anthony, Stanton teased, "I find there is no saying 'no' to you."[10]

Stanton's speech was an impassioned one and Anthony had fifty thousand copies of it made to give to politicians across the state. To the women's disappointment, though not to their surprise, the bill failed to pass.

TAKING HER SPEECHES ON THE ROAD

Believing more signatures were needed to persuade the reluctant men in the New York State Legislature, Susan B. Anthony decided to go on the road herself. On Christmas Day in 1854, she left for what would be a five month tour of towns and villages across the state.

It would be one of the coldest and snowiest winters on record. Anthony chose to travel in winter because she strategized that the state's many farmers could be more easily found in their homes than in the fields. She started her trip with $50 loaned to her by her friend Wendell Phillips, the famous abolitionist.

The money went quickly. Anthony charged a twenty-five cent entry fee to her speeches but she needed more. She had to place advertisements in local papers, buy train and carriage tickets, rent halls, and book inns. These logistics were challenging enough. The animosity she faced as a single female traveler made it even more difficult.

The cold was especially hard to take. Many of the rooms in the small inns where Anthony stayed had no fireplaces, and the blankets in the carriages did little to fight the frigid temperatures. Her feet got frostbite and her back went out. The back injury was so severe that for a while she had to be carried in and out of her speaking engagements.

Many people came to hear her. For some, the motivation was the sheer novelty of seeing a woman speaking in public. Yet for others, it was Susan B. Anthony and her message. One young woman gave this account:

> She talked plainly about our rights and how we ought to stand up for them and said the world would never go right until the women had just as much right to vote and rule as men. She asked us all to come up and sign our names who would promise to do all in our power to bring about that glad day…A whole lot of us went up and signed.[11]

When Anthony finally returned in May to her family's home in Rochester, she had spoken in nearly every county in the state. Five months of difficult relentless travel stood as evidence of her stamina and discipline. Anthony had kept a careful accounting of her expenses and had managed to save a bit of money. This she was already planning to use for her next campaign.

CHAPTER FOUR

WOMEN'S RIGHTS AND ABOLITIONISM

Susan B. Anthony's tireless trek crisscrossing New York State helped her land a new job. Persuaded by her grit, the American Anti-Slavery Society hired her to be its agent. They asked her to set up a statewide lecture tour for herself and others speaking out against slavery.

At $10 a week, the salary was meager but represented the first money Anthony would earn for reform work. Just as importantly, she would be permitted to continue her efforts for women's rights at the same time.

Elizabeth Cady Stanton was back in Seneca Falls with another baby, a second daughter. Over the next five years Stanton would rarely leave home, family obligations being what they were. Anthony was her essential tie to the outside movement.

Stanton was not the only women's activist with responsibilities at home. Antoinette Brown, the first woman to be ordained as a minister in the United States, had married the abolitionist Samuel Blackwell. Lucy Stone married Blackwell's brother Henry but kept her name, an unheard of act for the era.

In fact, as a single woman, Susan B. Anthony was a rare figure in the early women's movement. Most reformers were married and juggling home and children with meetings and conventions. In her usual blunt manner, Anthony sometimes appeared unsympathetic to their needs.

After Antoinette Brown Blackwell had her second child, Anthony wrote her, "I *say stop now*, once and for all. Your life work will be arduous enough with *two*."[1] When Lucy Stone got pregnant, Anthony withheld her congratulations, writing instead, "Lucy, *neither* of us have time for such *personal* matters."[2]

SPEAKING OUT AGAINST SLAVERY

For Anthony, nothing was more important than the cause before her. In 1857, few causes held more urgency than slavery. The Supreme Court had just fanned abolitionist fires with its decision in the Dred Scott case stating that slaves were not citizens and had no legal rights.

Anthony traveled throughout New York organizing engagements for every abolitionist she could convince to speak. She gave many lectures herself, describing slavery as "the Legalized, Systemic *robbery* of the *bodies* and *souls* of nearly *four millions* of men, women and children."[3]

These were not new ideas for Susan B. Anthony. She had been raised in a home that was a destination on the Underground Railroad. Frederick Douglass was a close family friend. Wendell Phillips had helped finance her petition campaign. But with the situation worsening every day in the country, Anthony stepped up her efforts.

This negative shows former slave and world-famous abolitionist Frederick Douglass in the years after the Civil War. Douglass was friendly with Susan B. Anthony's family and was a supporter of women's rights.

Then the abolitionist John Brown tried to raid an armory in Harpers Ferry, Virginia, in order to lead a rebellion of slaves. Brown was convicted of treason, the crime of betraying your country. He was hanged for his actions, and public sentiment was bitterly divided as to whether he was a hero or a criminal.

Angry groups of pro-slavery men began showing up at Anthony's speeches and heckling her. Braving this kind of hostility, Susan went to great lengths to publicize a meeting honoring John Brown. Three hundred people came to hear her celebrate his legacy.[4]

FRANCES WILLARD 1839–1898

President of the Woman's Christian Temperance Union, Frances Willard's motto was "do everything" and few women in the nineteenth century did more. Under her forceful leadership, the organization grew into one of the largest and most influential of the women's social reform movements. In 1876, in addition to its stance against alcohol, the Temperance Union began advocating for women's suffrage, bringing thousands of new activists to the cause.

MARRIAGE AND DIVORCE

During this same time, Anthony continued her advocacy for women's rights. In March 1860, she went to Albany, New York. The Married Woman's Property Act — the law she had canvassed for during the frigid winter — was finally coming up again for a vote before the state legislature.

This time the vote passed. The law in New York now provided that women had the right to own and inherit property, keep their earnings, enter into contracts, sue and be sued, and share custody of their children. Other states would soon follow New York's example.

The Married Woman's Property Act was the first great accomplishment of the young women's rights movement. Susan B. Anthony's unflagging efforts had made it possible. Two months later, the tenth annual National Woman's Rights Convention was held in New York City. Anthony opened the meetings with the joyful report of the group's recent legislative victory.

What happened next depended on whom you asked. Elizabeth Cady Stanton gave a speech that shocked her audience — some happily, others much less so. What is certain is that the speech put the convention hall in an uproar.

Stanton called for marriage to be redefined as a legal contract between two people. A contract that could be broken for reasons of drunkenness, cruelty, or abandonment. This was an idea that was ahead of its time.

In this era divorce was considered shameful and scandalous. Some of the convention delegates were uncomfortable with the topic even being discussed. Many viewed marriage as a religious covenant, an unbreakable agreement with God, not something that could be ended in a courtroom. Still others argued that divorce was not solely an issue for women.

Women in undesirable marriages usually had no choice but to stay with their husbands, even if their husbands were drunks and their lives were endangered. Women had no rights to their children and little hope of earning income.

Susan B. Anthony defended Stanton's argument and its inclusion on a women's rights agenda. But some other prominent advocates, Antoinette Brown, Lucy Stone, and Wendell Phillips among them, were stung. The controversy associated with Elizabeth Cady Stanton's speech and Susan B. Anthony's public support of it would last well beyond the convention.

Then a few months later there was more controversy. A woman named Phoebe Harris Phelps came to Susan B. Anthony seeking help in escaping her abusive husband, a prominent doctor and state senator in Massachusetts.

Phelps had confronted her husband with the evidence that he was cheating on her. After pushing her down a flight of stairs, Charles Phelps had his wife committed to an insane asylum where she was prohibited from seeing her children. After eighteen months of confinement, Phoebe Phelps managed to flee the institution and reunite with a daughter.

Despite the law in Massachusetts which still stated that a husband "owned" his wife and children, Susan B. Anthony escorted mother and daughter by train to New York City. They reached Manhattan late on Christmas night and began walking in the snow in a long search for a hotel that would give them a room without a man to accompany them.

WOMEN'S RIGHTS TAKE A BACK SEAT

The following day Anthony found a home for the Phelps women and returned upstate. There she was confronted by antislavery leaders William Lloyd Garrison and Wendell Phillips, who insisted she disclose the women's whereabouts. The abolitionists believed that their cause was being hurt by association with the case.

Susan B. Anthony refused to betray the women, though soon after they would be found and the father given full custody of the child. Anthony reminded Garrison and Phillips that she would no more return a slave to his imprisonment than a woman to hers. "Very many abolitionists," she wrote in her journal, "have yet to learn the ABCs of woman's rights."[5]

The antislavery and women's rights movements had supported each other for many years. After Elizabeth Cady Stanton's revolutionary stand on divorce and Susan B. Anthony's aid to a fugitive wife, the abolitionists' support grew shakier.

Then that April the world turned upside down for all Americans when President Abraham Lincoln declared Civil War. Citizen soldiers, including Anthony's two younger brothers, Daniel and Merritt, took to the battlefield and women's rights advocates temporarily suspended their cause for abolition.

The bloody war became a fearsome time to speak out against slavery. Even many Union supporters believed it was the abolitionists who had caused an uneasy balance to tip to war. Susan B. Anthony courageously faced angry mobs who cursed at her, threw eggs, doused the gas lamps during her speeches and even burned a stuffed cloth representation of her body.

While Anthony wholly supported abolition even when her life was threatened, she could see no good reason for taking a break from the fight for women's rights. To her mind, the women's cause was equally important. In addition, she worried about losing the momentum the movement had recently gained with the passage of the Married Woman's Property Act.

On this Anthony differed from others, including Elizabeth Cady Stanton. When Anthony argued for continuing the women's national conventions during wartime, her colleagues disagreed. Let us hold off for now, they advised. If we put all our support behind the Union cause, when the war ends with a Northern victory we will get abolitionist and congressional support in return.

Her hands tied without the backing of her comrades, Anthony returned to her family's home in Rochester. There she put to use on the farm the tremendous energy she normally spent advocating for reform. Her diary from this period includes entries like "washed every window in the house today" and "stained and varnished the library book-case today, and supervised the plowing of the orchard."[6]

TRIUMPH AND ANOTHER SETBACK

Anthony's concern that keeping quiet would lead to reversals for women was proved true. In 1862 the New York legislature stripped an essential provision from the Married Woman's Property Act that gave mothers equal custody of their children. "All we have gained," Anthony lamented, "thus snatched from us."[7]

Just weeks after this defeat, her grief grew more acute. Following a brief stomach illness, her father died. Daniel Anthony's influence on his daughter had been matched only by his devotion. From her father Susan learned at an early age the value of work and self-reliance. Daniel supported his daughter as a single woman and reformer at a time when both were unusual paths for a woman.

As was her way, Anthony turned to work to help her deal with her sadness. In the war's second year, Lincoln issued the Emancipation Proclamation, immediately freeing all slaves in the Confederacy but without doing the same for those in the North. The women's movement swiftly moved into action.

The National Woman's Loyal League was formed with Elizabeth Cady Stanton as president and Susan B. Anthony as secretary. Its mission was

CALL

FOR A MEETING OF THE

LOYAL WOMEN OF THE NATION.

In this crisis of our Country's destiny, it is the duty of every citizen to consider the peculiar blessings of a republican form of goverment and decide what sacrifices of wealth and life are demanded for its defence and preservation.

The policy of the war, our whole future life, depends on a universal, clearly defined idea of the end proposed, and the immense advantages to be secured to ourselves and all mankind, by its accomplishment.

No mere party or sectional cry, no technicalities of Constitution or military law, no mottoes of craft or policy are big enough to touch the great heart of a nation in the midst of revolution. A grand idea, such as freedom or justice, is needful to kindle and sustain the fires of a high enthusiasm.

At this hour, the best word and work of every man and woman are imperatively demanded. To man, by common consent, is assigned the forum, camp and field. What is woman's legitimate work, and how she may best accomplish it, is worthy our earnest counsel one with another.

We have heard many complaints of the lack of enthusiasm among Northern Women; but, when a mother lays her son on the altar of her country, she asks an object equal to the sacrifice. In nursing the sick and wounded, knitting socks, scraping lint, and making jellies, the bravest and best may weary if the thoughts mount not in faith to something beyond and above it all. Work is worship only when a noble purpose fills the soul.

Woman is equally interested and responsible with man in the final settlement of this problem of self-government; therefore let none stand idle spectators now. When every hour is big with destiny, and each delay but complicates our difficulties, it is high time for the daughters of the revolution, in solemn council, to unseal the last will and testament of the Fathers,—lay hold of their birthright of freedom, and keep it a sacred trust for all coming generations.

To this end, we ask the loyal Women of the Nation to meet in New York, on Thursday, the 14th of May next.

Let the Women of every State be largely represented, both by person and by letter.

There will be two sessions — The first at 10 o'clock, A. M., at the Church of the Puritans, (Dr Cheever's), Admittance Free—The second at the Cooper Institute—at 7½ o'clock, P. M., Admittance 25 cents.   On behalf of the Woman's Central Committee,

ELIZABETH CADY STANTON.

N. B.—Communications relative to and for the meeting should be addressed to SUSAN B. ANTHONY, 48 Beekman St., New York.

During the Civil War Susan B. Anthony and her fellow suffragists tabled their fight. However, Anthony and Cady Stanton organized the National Women's Loyal League in 1863, in an effort to abolish slavery.

simple but monumental: to collect a million signatures to a petition asking Congress to pass the
Thirteenth Amendment abolishing slavery.

For fifteen months league members, including
more than two thousand volunteers, worked dili-
gently. Susan B. Anthony survived on a tiny stipend
that allowed her only ten cents a day for lunch.[8] As
the signatures multiplied, the paper rolls they were
written on got bigger and bigger. Eventually over
four hundred thousand signatures were obtained.
The work of the Woman's Loyal League was
instrumental in convincing Congress to pass the
amendment.

Anthony and Stanton were gratified by their
group's accomplishment not only because it helped
pass the antislavery amendment but also because
they trusted that it would help advance women's
rights. To Anthony and Stanton, the rights of slaves
and women could be linked in a common cause.

The war ended and the Southern states
rejoined the Union. With abolition achieved, its
advocates turned to voting rights. An amendment
to the US Constitution was proposed, broadening
the franchise to former slaves. The women would
have to wait, Wendell Phillips said, it was first "the
Negro's hour."[9]

Wendell Phillips was a longtime supporter of
women's rights. It was not that he was unsympathetic to the cause but rather that he was a
hard-nosed political strategist. Phillips believed

that it was going to be difficult enough to find the votes in Congress for the freed slaves. Adding women to the mix would complicate the issue for him and his colleagues.

Susan B. Anthony and Elizabeth Cady Stanton were furious. After all the support the women's movement had given to the abolitionist cause they believed they should receive their cooperation. Moreover, they questioned, did the abolitionists somehow fail to notice that many slaves were also women?

Anthony and Stanton quickly got back to work. They directed a petition campaign that collected ten thousand signatures asking Congress to include women in the suffrage amendment. But not only did they fail to bring any congressmen to their side, they discovered something even more worrisome.

For the first time ever, the proposed constitutional amendment was to include a gender distinction. A citizen of the United States was suddenly being defined as a *male* citizen. Pandemonium was about to break loose in the women's rights movement.

CHAPTER FIVE

A DIVISIVE BATTLE

W hen Susan B. Anthony wanted to continue the push for women's rights during the Civil War, her coworkers had urged otherwise and overruled her. Now with the war over, it appeared clear that the support Anthony's colleagues had predicted was not going to be forthcoming.

Neither the abolitionists nor the newly victorious Union supporters were willing to give the women their due. Abolition reformers saw their main loyalty as being with the freed slaves. Women will get the vote in time, they argued, suffrage should first go to black men.

From the point of view of the Union supporters in Congress, giving black men the vote was a smart move. The freedmen would provide millions of new votes to their side. On the other hand, giving women the vote would have to include Southern white women. Giving them the vote would have the exact opposite effect.

When the proposed Fourteenth Amendment not only failed to say anything about voting for women but expressly defined citizens as "male," women's rights advocates were devastated. The amendment appeared to raise the issue of whether women were actually citizens of the United States.

Elizabeth Cady Stanton fumed that the amendment would set back the women's suffrage movement one hundred years.[1] It is perhaps no coincidence that largely from this point forward, advocates began referring to their cause explicitly as women's suffrage rather than women's rights.[2]

The Fourteenth Amendment continued to be debated; the language defining citizens as male. In fact, however, the amendment would not provide freedmen with the right to vote. The abolition reformers would need to continue their efforts.

Still hoping that what some were calling "the negro's hour" could be the woman's hour as well, suffrage activists formed a new organization called the American Equal Rights Association. The association's main goal was to unite the efforts for black suffrage with those for women's suffrage.

Yet from the very start, the members of the association were at odds. Susan B. Anthony and Elizabeth Cady Stanton maintained that nothing less than universal suffrage must be made into law. Lucy Stone and Antoinette Brown allied with Frederick Douglass and Wendell Phillips. Their side was open to giving black men the vote as an initial step.

New-York, December 26, 1865.

Dear Friend:

As the question of Suffrage is now agitating the public mind, it is the hour for Woman to make her demand.

Propositions have already been made on the floor of Congress to so amend the Constitution as to exclude Women form a voice in the Government.* As this would be to turn the wheels of legislation backward, let the Women of the Nation now unitedly protest against such a desecration of the Constitution, and petition for that right which is at the foundation of all Government, the right of representation.

Send your petition, when signed, to your representative in Congress, at your earliest convenience.

Address all communications to

Standard Office, 48 Beekman St., New York.

In behalf of the National W. R. Com.

E. CADY STANTON,
S. B. ANTHONY,
LUCY STONE.

* See Bill of Mr. Jenckes, of Rhode Island.

With the war over, Anthony could get back to her cause. In December 1865, along with Elizabeth Cady Stanton and Lucy Stone, she called on their friends to petition their congressmen in support of women's suffrage.

IDA B. WELLS-BARNETT 1862–1931

Ida B. Wells-Barnett was born into slavery six months before the Emancipation Proclamation was signed. At twenty-two she was forced to sit in a segregated train car, and subsequently won a lawsuit against the railroad. As an editor and journalist for the *Memphis Free Speech*, her courageous series of reports on lynching led to mob attacks at the newspaper and threats on her life. In 1893 she stayed overnight at Susan B. Anthony's home. When a typist working for Anthony refused to help Wells-Barnett because she was black, Anthony fired her on the spot. After settling in Chicago, Ida Wells-Barnett founded the first kindergarten for black children and the Alpha Suffrage Club, the first black women's suffrage organization.

A CONTROVERSIAL ALLIANCE

During this same period, for the first time a state was planning to vote on women's suffrage. Kansas, which had become a state just six years earlier, was still working on its own constitution. Lucy Stone and her husband, Henry Blackwell, traveled there to drum up support.

In the early fall, Susan B. Anthony and Elizabeth Cady Stanton joined them. In 1867, Kansas was still the frontier. Settlements were few and far between and accommodations primitive. Yet Anthony relished the experience, writing, "We are getting along splendidly. Just the frame of a Methodist church with sidings and a roof, and rough cottonwood boards for seats, was our meeting place last night here."[3]

The Kansas campaign however, was not getting along as splendidly. The funding that the women had always been able to count on from the antislavery base had stopped. When money was offered to them from an unlikely source, Anthony and Stanton decided to take it.

Their supporter was a man named George Francis Train. He was an eccentric loudmouth. He was very wealthy, having earned millions in shipping and railroads. He loved flashy clothes, including lavender gloves he was seldom seen without. He was pro-slavery and planned to run for president one day. He was also an ardent believer in women's rights.

Train had come to the attention of a few members of Congress who supported women's suffrage. His considerable financial resources were hard to resist but someone had to keep his racist rhetoric in check. The congressmen believed that Susan B. Anthony was the just the strong-willed person they needed to control Train.[4]

George Francis Train offered to fund a newspaper devoted to suffrage. His alliance was controversial.

Anthony was not aware of the congressmen's scheming but took to the campaign trail with Train for the final two weeks before the state legislature's vote. Kansas would overwhelmingly defeat the suffrage measure but George Francis Train vowed to keep the fight going.

His first plan was for Anthony and Stanton to accompany him on a pro-suffrage lecture tour, all expenses paid. The trio stayed at fancy hotels and ate in only the finest restaurants. The second opportunity he offered them was even better. Train proposed to finance a weekly newspaper supporting suffrage.

A newspaper of their own was something Anthony and Stanton had wanted for a long time. Susan B. Anthony managed the business end while Elizabeth Cady Stanton served as editor. They decided to call their paper the *Revolution.* Its motto was "Men, their rights and nothing more; women, their rights and nothing less!"

The *Revolution*'s first edition appeared just a month after Train made his offer. It included a report of a meeting Susan B. Anthony had with President Andrew Johnson in which she lobbied him for the women's vote.[5] As the paper's proprietor, Anthony worked with her typical high-energy, selling advertising and subscriptions and overseeing operational costs like printing and office rent.

The sixteen-page weekly made an extraordinary contribution to the women's cause. It was almost entirely staffed by

The Revolution gave Anthony and Stanton the chance to push their agenda back into the spotlight after the Civil War.

women. It carried news about women from all walks of life that no other newspaper deemed worthy. Its editorials rallied against discrimination in women's lives. And it campaigned tirelessly for women's suffrage.[6]

George Francis Train not only left Anthony and Stanton alone to run their paper, he left the country and ended up in an English jail for his support of Irish independence. After two years, his financial backing ended and the *Revolution* was in too much debt to continue. It would take Susan B. Anthony seven years to pay off the paper's creditors.

Despite the difficulties when the paper went under, Anthony cherished her work at the *Revolution.* She wrote a friend, "I have the joy of knowing that I showed it to be possible to publish an out-and-out woman's paper, and taught other women to enter in and reap where I have sown."[7]

THE ALIENATING REVOLUTION

Not everyone associated with the women's movement felt the same about the newspaper. Many found fault with its content. The *Revolution* regularly discussed controversial subjects like divorce and prostitution. Its editorials defiantly criticized all who refused to back universal suffrage. Others viewed with horror the paper's association with the bigoted George Francis Train.

A group led by Lucy Stone, Antoinette Brown Blackwell, and Wendell Phillips publicly distanced themselves from Susan B. Anthony and Elizabeth Cady Stanton. Stone proclaimed, "We are now in the midst of a serious quarrel with Miss Anthony and Mrs. Stanton."[8]

After a bitter ratification fight in the former Confederate states, the Fourteenth Amendment was passed, promising former slaves equal protection under the law. Yet no real protection existed from the murderous acts of racist groups like the newly formed Ku Klux Klan. A Fifteenth Amendment providing freedmen the vote was hurriedly proposed.

Lucy Stone's group of abolitionists and women's activists supported the Fifteenth Amendment. As before, they were willing to delay women's suffrage for what they believed was a necessary first-step response to the abomination of slavery.

As they had before, Susan B. Anthony and Elizabeth Cady Stanton wholeheartedly disagreed with any suffrage amendment which did not include women. Congress passed the Fifteenth Amendment, and the familiar debate grew even more resentful.

For the first time, a formal split took place in the women's movement. Two separate organizations were established. While both groups viewed their ultimate goal as getting women the vote, they had different ideas on how to best accomplish it.

Lucy Stone and her allies founded the American Woman Suffrage Association. The group's mission was directed solely toward the cause of suffrage. Men were invited to join and in fact a man became its first president. The association started a newspaper called the *Woman's Journal*.

Susan B. Anthony and Elizabeth Cady Stanton, along with their followers, established the National Woman Suffrage Association, which they called simply The National. For them, suffrage came first but associated issues like divorce and improved conditions for working women were also important. The National was open to anyone who paid $1 to join, but men were not permitted to hold office.

The biggest difference between the rival organizations centered on their political strategy. Lucy Stone's group was open to the idea of women's suffrage laws passing state-by-state. Having pushed hard and unsuccessfully for the vote in Kansas and New York, Anthony and Stanton wanted nothing less than a national constitutional amendment.

From the start, Susan B. Anthony was responsible for planning The National's twice yearly conventions. She set the agenda and booked the speakers. She rented the hall and always furnished the stage to resemble a comfortable living room, complete with rugs, sofas, and potted plants. Then she took full charge of the meetings. A newspaper account described her this way:

> Miss Anthony is the ruling spirit of the convention. She dominates. She is constantly on the alert and has a keen appreciation of every point made by a speaker. She lets no point pass without emphasizing it and impressing it upon the convention.[9]

In an era when most women were still afraid to speak in public, Susan B. Anthony was a confident,

At first, Victoria Woodhull seemed to be a valuable addition to the suffragist cause, but she was deemed too radical to help. Woodhull later ran as a candi-

accomplished orator and meeting chairperson. "The woman suffragists love her for her good works," a reporter noted, "the audience for her brightness and wit, and the press for her frank, plain, open, business-like way."[10]

At the National's second meeting, Anthony acted quickly to avert a near debacle. Anthony had invited a woman named Victoria Woodhull to address the convention. Woodhull was a passionate supporter of women's rights but also of free love, the idea that people should be allowed to have sex outside of marriage. This idea was a radical one for the day.

When Victoria Woodhull went from urging for women's suffrage to clamoring for free love and her own aspirations to be president of the United States, Susan B. Anthony thought on her feet. Resolved that no person was going to take over the convention for her own purposes, Anthony turned out the lights in the convention hall and cut off her speaker.

Afterwards, Anthony addressed the controversy of Woodhull's appearance. She stopped the speech, she explained, because Woodhull put personal ambitions before the cause. Still, Susan B. Anthony warned, women must never be afraid to hear opposing viewpoints. "Cautious, careful people always casting about to preserve their reputation or social standards can never bring about reform."[11]

CHAPTER SIX

A BOLD MOVE

To bring support to the suffrage cause and to help pay back the *Revolution*'s debt of ten thousand dollars, Susan B. Anthony took to the lecture circuit. With Elizabeth Cady Stanton joining her and financing the trip, the pair embarked on a cross-country tour aboard the new transcontinental railroad.

The train line was the first to extend its tracks all the way west to California. The women traveled in a first-class car and it was a luxurious way to go. Sleeping cars or Pullmans, as they were called after the engineer who designed them, featured comfortable seating areas and beds, as well as elegant dining rooms.

Stopping regularly to speak, often before large audiences, the press followed them with interest. After hearing Anthony address the crowds in Denver, a reporter wrote admiringly, "if one-half of her sex possessed one-half of her acquirements, her intellectual culture, her self-reliance and independence of character, the world would be better for it."[1]

This woodcut depicts suffragist and journalist Laura deForce Gordon and Susan B. Anthony being escorted to speak in Cincinnati in the 1870s. Anthony embarked on the lecture circuit to spread the word about suffrage.

One of Anthony's most famous lectures was entitled "Woman Wants Bread, Not the Ballot." In this speech, which she presented more than one hundred times, she argued that of course the reality is just the opposite, "that the only possibility of her securing bread and a home for herself is to give her the ballot."[2]

The two-hour talk ended with an eloquent call to action. "Carry out the spirit of our Constitution, put into the hands of all women, as you have into those of all men, the ballot, that symbol of perfect equality, the right protective of all other rights."[3]

DRIVEN OUT OF CALIFORNIA

What had been an entirely enjoyable and successful trip turned sour when the women got to San Francisco. All was fine at the outset. They were given a suite at the Grand Hotel and were taken sailing in the bay.

It was after a prison visit to a prostitute named Laura Fair that things started to get ugly. Fair had been charged with killing her client, a prominent attorney. Believing there were two sides to every story, Susan and Elizabeth went to speak with her.

When Anthony tried to give a scheduled lecture the following day, she was shouted down by an angry crowd. She held her ground, arguing "if all men had protected all women as they would have their own wives and daughters protected, you would have no Laura Fair in your jail tonight."[4]

The San Francisco newspapers expressed their contempt next. Anthony was attacked for her unspoken approval of prostitution and even murder. All her speaking engagements in California were cancelled on the spot. That night she wrote in her journal, "Never in all my hard experience have I been under such fire."[5]

CASTING A VOTE

While Elizabeth Cady Stanton returned home to take care of her dying mother, Susan B. Anthony pressed on alone. Since she could no longer lecture in California, she decided to go to the Oregon and Washington territories instead. Without Stanton there to pay her expenses, Anthony went by stagecoach and ferry, much rougher means of travel.

Throughout the Northwest, Susan B. Anthony put forth a new justification for women's suffrage. A married couple named Virginia and Francis Minor had recently argued before a lower court that women already had the right to vote under the Fourteenth Amendment. Women were citizens too, they noted simply, therefore their vote was guaranteed by the amendment.

Among suffrage advocates, the Minors' reasoning became known as the "New Departure." If higher courts upheld this argument, the long fight for the women's vote would finally be over. In her speeches in the western territories, Anthony urged women to test the case by voting in the upcoming presidential election.

Susan B. Anthony planned to be among the women voting. She had wanted to try and vote before but had been held back by the simple fact that she was never living at her legal address, her parent's home in Rochester, for the thirty-day period immediately preceding election day. The thirty-day residency was a requirement of New York State law. This year she made sure to return to Rochester with sufficient time.

On November 1, 1872, Susan and her three sisters, Guelma, Mary, and Hannah, went to register to vote at a barbershop that was serving double duty as a registry office. When the election inspectors immediately turned them down, Anthony argued their right to vote as citizens defined under the Fourteenth Amendment.

Having considered before she made her case that the legal argument alone might not sway officials, Susan had a plan B. She told the inspectors that not only had she hired the best lawyer in town to defend herself, she would also cover any fines the men might receive by registering them.[6]

Anthony's shrewd strategy paid off. Susan and her sisters were allowed to register to vote and ten other women also did the same after them. The *Rochester Union and Advertiser* would scoff in its editorial three days later, "Citizenship no more carries the right to vote than it carries the power to fly to the moon."[7]

On election day, November 5, Susan B. Anthony cast a ballot for Ulysses S. Grant and at once dashed off a letter to Elizabeth Cady Stanton. "Well I have been and gone and done it!!" she wrote with great excitement. "Positively voted the Republican ticket strait this a.m. at 7 o'clock."[8]

Anthony's voting made headlines across the country. A small group of women had been defying the law by registering and voting for the last four years. When Susan B. Anthony voted however, it was big news.

ROSE SCHNEIDERMAN 1882–1972

A Polish immigrant and cap maker by trade, Rose Schneiderman helped bring together women's issues in the union and suffrage causes. She understood the importance of the women's vote in compelling Congress to pass proactive legislation for working women. As a leader in the International Ladies' Garment Workers' Union, she advocated for the eight-hour work day and minimum wage laws. As a member of the National Woman Suffrage Association, Schneiderman canvassed throughout Ohio and helped Susan B. Anthony with the campaign in New York State.

ARREST AND TRIAL

Three weeks later, a United States deputy marshal rang the doorbell at the Anthony home. With a timid manner, he asked Susan if she would please go to the office of Commissioner William C. Storrs. When Anthony confirmed with the marshal that this request meant she was being arrested, she held out her wrists and demanded to be handcuffed as any man would be.

Her trial was set for the following June. Anthony spent the months in between giving lectures in every one of the small towns in the county in which she was to be tried. Her speech was titled "Is It A Crime For A Citizen Of The United States To Vote?" Anthony's talk was so persuasive the prosecuting attorney believed she had convinced all her listeners of her cause. He had the trial changed to another county.

On the opening day of her trial, Susan B. Anthony found the courtroom filled to capacity. Her case would be the first one that Justice

Judge Ward Hunt presided over the trial of Susan B. Anthony, flagrantly violating her constitutional rights.

Ward Hunt would be hearing as a federal judge. Hunt owed his new job to a senator who was adamantly opposed to women's rights. From the very start, it was clear that the trial would be a sham.

Anthony lawyer was Henry R. Selden, a former judge and longtime friend. When Selden tried to call Anthony as a witness on her own behalf, the prosecution and judge disallowed it. As a woman, they claimed, she was incompetent to testify.

When the lawyers for both sides finished presenting their cases, Judge Hunt took from his pocket a paper with an opinion that he had prepared before the trial even began. The Fourteenth Amendment did not cover the defendant's right to vote, he declared. Without even allowing the jury to deliberate, he instructed them to find her guilty.

The next day Henry Selden argued for a new trial on the grounds that Anthony's constitutional right to a trial by jury had been violated. Judge Hunt denied the motion and asked Anthony if she had anything to say.

With her usual forceful eloquence, Susan B. Anthony addressed the judge. Though he quickly ordered her to stop speaking, she went on at great length. "You have trampled under foot every vital principle of our government, " she said in part. "I am degraded from the status of citizen to that of a subject; and not only myself individually, but all of my sex."[9]

At the trial's conclusion, the judge fined Anthony $100 dollars plus court costs. When she refused to pay any of it, he refused as well to jail her for it. His move was a calculated one to prevent her from appealing to the Supreme Court, which might have been permitted had the judge imprisoned her until the fine was paid.

That night Anthony wrote in her journal, "the greatest judicial outrage history ever recorded!"[10]

Yet ever the brilliant strategist, Anthony had three thousand copies of the trial proceedings printed up and distributed, exposing the kangaroo court for what it was.

As one New York newspaper commented afterward, "Miss Anthony is still ahead. She has voted and the American constitution has survived the shock. Fining her one hundred dollars does not rule out the fact that…women voted, and went home, and the world jogged on as before."[11]

CHAPTER SEVEN

THE NEAREST EXAMPLE OF PERPETUAL MOTION

While Susan B. Anthony may have caused the biggest stir across America with her vote in the 1872 presidential election, another woman's attempt to vote carried with it greater legal consequences.

Virginia Minor, the president of the Woman Suffrage Association of Missouri, went to vote in St. Louis. She and her husband, Francis, an attorney, were the ones who had introduced the "New Departure," the legal argument that the Fourteenth Amendment gave women the right to vote.

When Virginia Minor was prevented from registering she decided to sue the registrar, a man named Reese Happersett. Since as a married woman in Missouri she was not permitted to bring a suit herself, she did so in partnership with her husband.

Minor v. Happersett went all the way to the United States Supreme Court. In 1875, the court unanimously ruled against Virginia Minor.

It said that the citizenship provided under the Fourteenth Amendment did not also confer the right to vote. The court held too that each state had the right to decide who could vote within its borders.

After the decision in the Minor case, Lucy Stone's American Woman Suffrage Association stepped up its efforts to get women the vote with a campaign aimed at changing state constitutions. Susan B. Anthony's National Woman Suffrage Association took a different tack, pushing Congress hard for a Sixteenth Amendment to the constitution.

Virginia Minor's lawsuit against a Missouri registrar for preventing her from voting went all the way to the US Supreme Court.

Yet while Anthony always kept faith that constitutional change would happen one day, she never stopped working at the state level, addressing legislatures and speaking to their constituencies.

SEIZING AN OPPORTUNITY

1876 marked the nation's centennial. Six months of commemorative patriotic events were on the government's calendar, culminating in an elaborate Fourth of July celebration in Philadelphia. The women's movement was not invited to participate in any of the festivities.

Incensed by their exclusion, the National Woman Suffrage Association first came up with the idea that its members parade wearing all black and carrying protest banners. In the end, a more positive and comprehensive plan won out.

In May, they set up headquarters in an office near the fairgrounds in downtown Philadelphia. As a single woman and thus the only woman who was legally permitted, Anthony signed the lease.

For the next few weeks, she worked along-side Elizabeth Cady Stanton and Matilda Joslyn Gage, another leader in the reform movement. The trio drafted a "Declaration of Rights for Women." In some ways, this document differed from the one with the similar name that Elizabeth Cady Stanton had presented at the Seneca Falls Convention. After nearly thirty years, the women's movement had made some real progress. Many women were now keeping their earnings, speaking in public, and getting an education.

In other ways, this new "Declaration of Rights" echoed 1848. In a democracy, it argued, voting was the primary method by which people delegated authority to their representatives. Since women still could not vote, it continued, women were not represented by their government.

It appeared that women were not going to be represented on the dais at the official centennial celebration either. The National's request to address the Fourth of July gathering was turned down by the planning committee. A request for tickets was denied as well.

In a savvy countermove, Susan B. Anthony got press passes for the women through her brother, who published a newspaper in Kansas. While they could not sit on the speaker's platform, she reasoned, they could still make their presence felt.

July 4th was a steamy, hot day. The ceremonies began with Richard Henry Lee, a descendant of one of the original signers, reading aloud the US Declaration of Independence. As he concluded, Susan stood up and walked to the main stage. She handed a rolled parchment copy of the women's declaration to the vice president of the United States who bowed to her as he received it.

Anthony then turned and left the hall. Standing outside, under an umbrella that Matilda Joslyn Gage held to shield her from the

DECLARATION OF RIGHTS

OF THE

WOMEN OF THE UNITED STATES

BY THE

NATIONAL WOMAN SUFFRAGE ASSOCIATION,

JULY 4th, 1876.

WHILE the Nation is buoyant with patriotism, and all hearts are attuned to praise, it is with sorrow we come to strike the one discordant note, on this hundredth anniversary of our country's birth. When subjects of Kings, Emperors, and Czars, from the Old World, join in our National Jubilee, shall the women of the Republic refuse to lay their hands with benedictions on the nation's head? Surveying America's Exposition, surpassing in magnificence those of London, Paris, and Vienna, shall we not rejoice at the success of the youngest rival among the nations of the earth? May not our hearts, in unison with all, swell with pride at our great achievements as a people; our free speech, free press, free schools, free church, and the rapid progress we have made in material wealth, trade, commerce, and the inventive arts? And we do rejoice, in the success thus far, of our experiment of self-government. Our faith is firm and unwavering in the broad principles of human rights, proclaimed in 1776, not only as abstract truths, but as the corner stones of a republic. Yet, we cannot forget, even in this glad hour, that while all men of every race, and clime, and condition, have been invested with the full rights of citizenship, under our hospitable flag, all women still suffer the degradation of disfranchisement.

The history of our country the past hundred years, has been a series of assumptions and usurpations of power over woman, in direct opposition to the principles of just government, acknowledged by the United States at its foundation, which are:

First. The natural rights of each individual.

Second. The exact equality of these rights.

Third. That these rights, when not delegated by the individual, are retained by the individual.

Fourth. That no person can exercise the rights of others without delegated authority.

Fifth. That the non-use of these rights does not destroy them.

And for the violation of these fundamental principles of our Government, we arraign our rulers on this 4th day of July, 1876,—and these are our

ARTICLES OF IMPEACHMENT.

BILLS OF ATTAINDER have been passed by the introduction of the word "male" into all the State constitutions, denying to woman the right of suffrage, and thereby making sex a crime—an exercise of power clearly forbidden in Article 1st, Sections 9th and 10th of the United States Constitution.

With Matilda Joslyn Gage and Elizabeth Cady Stanton, Anthony drafted a Declaration of Rights of the Women of the United States. Their point was that the government was infringing on their rights.

intense sun, Susan B. Anthony read aloud the Declaration of Rights for Women. A large cheering crowd gathered and heard her ask that "all the civil and political rights that belong to citizens of the United States, be guaranteed to us and our daughters forever."[1]

HISTORY OF WOMAN SUFFRAGE

A month after the successful Philadelphia Centennial, the three authors of its women's declaration reunited at Elizabeth Cady Stanton's stately home in Tenafly, New Jersey. The women planned to roll up their sleeves and begin work on a major project, a history of the women's suffrage movement.

At the outset, the women believed they could complete the history in four months. What would end up becoming a six-volume series would in fact take them many years to finish.

While firmly believing in the project, a naturally restless Susan B. Anthony found it agonizing to actually sit still and write it.[2]

Anthony had compiled scrapbooks and kept boxes full of newspaper clippings, letters, and reports for many years. Organizing these alone was a gigantic task. In addition, she managed the business end of the project, finding a publisher and arranging for the book's distribution to libraries and schools.

To date, *History of Woman Suffrage* remains the encyclopedic primary source on the subject. It almost did not get written. For Susan B. Anthony and Elizabeth Cady Stanton, collaborating on the book was as demanding and enriching as their friendship. Stanton's eldest daughter, Margaret, provided an intimate account of a typical work day for the women.

> They start off pretty well in the morning, fresh and amiable. They write page after page with alacrity, they laugh and talk, poke the fire by turn, and admire the flowers I place on their desk...suddenly I hear a hot dispute about something. ...down go the pens, one sails out one door and one out the other...When they return they go straight to work where they left off, as if nothing happened.[3]

The main reason why the *History of Woman Suffrage* took as long as it did to get finished was because its authors were always very busy. For nine months in 1877 Anthony was back on the road giving lectures throughout the Midwest and plains states.

She traveled by stagecoach and horse-drawn wagon. Most of the territory she covered was rough and sparsely populated. The inns she stayed at

Anthony and Elizabeth Cady Stanton worked together to write the four-volume *History of Woman Suffrage*. Were it not for this detailed record, much of the early history of the women's rights movement might have been lost.

served salt-pork for both meals and had bedbugs in their mattresses. Yet though she was fifty-seven years old, Anthony showed no signs of slowing down. Stanton described her as "the nearest example of perpetual motion."[4]

ALICE PAUL 1885–1977

The daughter of a suffrage activist, Alice Paul became a radical reformer for the cause, unafraid to use more confrontational tactics to get a suffrage amendment passed. Paul organized a march of eight thousand women's suffrage supporters, at that time the largest parade ever held in Washington, DC. For eighteen months she and other "silent sentinels" picketed the White House, never speaking but carrying banners with inflammatory messages. Arrested and jailed for seven months, she went on a hunger strike and was force-fed. In 1919 President Wilson finally gave his support to women's suffrage. Until her death, Alice Paul would advocate tirelessly but ultimately unsuccessfully for an Equal Rights Amendment to the constitution.

A TIRELESS CAMPAIGN

In January 1878, Senator Arlen Sargent of California, a close friend of Susan B. Anthony's, introduced a Sixteenth Amendment in Congress. It read simply, "The right of citizens to vote shall not be denied or abridged by the United States or by any State on account of sex." Very few of Sargent's colleagues supported it but the bill soon became known by a popular nickname, the Susan B. Anthony Amendment.

Susan B. Anthony continued to organize and run the annual convention for the National Woman Suffrage Association in Washington, DC. Keeping the convention in the nation's capitol was no accident. Every winter while they were in town, Anthony pushed attendees to lobby members of Congress.

Any progress the movement made seemed always to come at a snail's pace. The Senate finally agreed to appoint a small subcommittee on women's suffrage. Susan gave each member of the committee a copy of the first volume of the *History of Woman Suffrage.*

Then when the meetings in Washington were over, Anthony went back to campaigning state-by-state. The work was repetitive and punishing. Susan was often alone while she traveled. Her family back in Rochester was growing smaller as well, with the deaths of her sister Hannah and her mother within three years of one another.

In 1883, Susan B. Anthony allowed herself a rare break from routine and sailed to London, where Elizabeth Cady Stanton had been living with her daughter for six months. Susan had never before been abroad. Newspapers on both sides of the Atlantic reported on her trip.

A young woman named Rachel Foster accompanied Anthony as her assistant. Only twenty-five, Foster was a hard-working advocate for suffrage and part of a group of young women known as "Susan's girls."[5] To the members of this select group, Anthony was "Aunt Susan." Susan B. Anthony enjoyed and took very seriously her role as mentor.

For nine months, Anthony and Foster traveled throughout Europe. While they did some sight-seeing, meetings with suffrage activists and political leaders took priority. In Paris, Anthony did allow herself one treat: "my continental breakfast — rolls, butter and coffee — was sent to my room and, for the first time in my life, I ate it in bed. What would my mother have said?"[6]

By year's end Anthony's tenacious work ethic was making her fidgety. It was time to sail home and get back to work.

CHAPTER EIGHT

CHANGING A MINORITY INTO A MAJORITY

On the second day of the National Woman Suffrage Association's annual convention in 1887, word came that the Senate was finally going to vote on the Sixteenth Amendment. Convention delegates rushed over to the Capitol building where they could observe the vote from the Senate gallery.

It had taken eleven years just for the amendment to get to a vote by the full Senate. In short order it was defeated, 34 to 16. Back on the convention floor the National passed a resolution, "that when a new Congress shall have assembled, with new men and new ideas, we may hope to change this minority into a majority."[1]

The National chose to put a positive spin on the amendment's defeat, and a small but worthy victory for the cause had just been won out West. The new state of Wyoming was to become the first in the United States to give women the vote.

COMING TOGETHER

In truth, however, by the end of the 1880s —over forty years after the first rights convention in Seneca Falls — the women's suffrage movement needed more than optimism. It appeared it was time to put aside differences and harness all forces.

In February 1890, the National and American Woman Suffrage associations merged into one, the National American Woman Suffrage Association, or NAWSA. Elizabeth Cady Stanton was elected president and Susan B. Anthony its vice president.

The reunification might never have happened had it been left to the original founders. Instead, the younger generation of the women's movement negotiated terms. Likely it helped their discussions that none of them had been around at the time of the nasty split.

Susan B. Anthony's "niece," Rachel Foster, represented the National during the merger talks. Anthony had been grooming Rachel as her possible successor when she learned that Foster had secretly adopted a baby girl.

That Rachel Foster had elected to become a single mother, a shocking choice to most in that era, did not matter to Anthony at all. Susan was only concerned that motherhood would make Foster less available to the cause. Rachel Foster would marry the following year, becoming Rachel Foster Avery and remaining active in the movement.

Susan B. Anthony, Rachel Foster Avery.
Copyright by the
Mary F. Seymour Publishing Company, 1890.

Susan B. Anthony was photographed with her protégé Rachel Foster Avery in 1890. Avery remained active in the women's movement despite Anthony's fears that her family would detract from her availability.

ELIZABETH GURLEY FLYNN 1890–1964

Raised by activist parents, Elizabeth Gurley Flynn was first arrested at sixteen while advocating for socialism on a street corner in New York City. As an organizer for the Industrial Workers of the World, she defended restaurant cooks, coal miners, and textile workers. An ardent supporter of both women's suffrage and the peace movement during World War I, she was arrested and charged with spying. The espionage case was dropped but Elizabeth Gurley Flynn sued for her right to free speech and in 1920 helped found the American Civil Liberties Union. Flynn's activism would continue for the rest of her life and include a two-year prison term for being a member of the Communist Party.

STILL TRAVELING THE COUNTRY

Susan B. Anthony turned seventy years old. Two hundred guests honored her with a dinner in Washington, DC. Her dark hair had become gray, but her health was still excellent. While she continued with a travel schedule that would prove strenuous even for a younger person, the appeal of home had grown greater for her as well.

Elizabeth Cady Stanton's husband had died, and Susan proposed that Elizabeth come live with her in Rochester. Stanton decided against it, moving instead into a large apartment in New York City with two of her adult children.

She came to stay with Susan soon after. Marble busts of Anthony, Stanton, and Lucretia Mott had been commissioned for exhibition at the upcoming World's Columbian Exposition in Chicago. Anthony arranged for the sculptor to come to Rochester, and the women took turns posing for her.

Sitting long hours for an artist was difficult for Susan B. Anthony. Even in her seventies, her high energy persisted. New York was again amending its constitution, so once again Anthony went and pushed for suffrage across the state. The bill's repeat defeat was a huge disappointment.[2]

The Chicago Exposition cheered her up. The world's first Ferris wheel was on display and William "Buffalo Bill" Cody had brought his famous Wild West Show. Anthony attended the performance with friends who reported, "He rode directly to our boxes, reined his horse in front of Miss Anthony, rose in his stirrups, and with his characteristic gesture swept his slouch-hat to his saddle-bow in salutation."[3]

From Chicago she continued west to Kansas. There, as in New York, the state revisited and again defeated a suffrage bill. The news from

Colorado was much better. A young activist named Carrie Chapman Catt helped lead the successful campaign there. Susan described herself as "the happiest woman in America."[4]

California had a suffrage bill scheduled for a vote the following year. Advocates there asked Anthony to come out and help them canvass the state. In every city she stopped in along the way, friends and supporters celebrated her seventy-fifth birthday.

Rachel Foster Avery surprised her with a gift fund that provided her $800 a year. Avery had secretly collected from almost two hundred contributors and invested the money. For the first time in her life, Anthony had financial security.

In California, Susan allowed herself a few days of vacation. She went to Yosemite National Park in the Sierra Nevada Mountains. She put on bloomers and rode on a mule. A ranger officially named one of the trees in the park after her. Anna Howard Shaw, a younger suffrage activist, accompanied her. The two women stayed in the state for six weeks, speaking on suffrage and working to design a campaign.

On the trip back East, Anthony fainted while giving a speech in Ohio. Rumors spread at once that she was near death. An editor from a Chicago newspaper telegraphed his reporter to write "5000 words if still living, no limit if dead."[5] Anthony wasn't dead. She spent the rest of the summer recovering at the home of a friend.

Anna Howard Shaw was a suffragist, physician, and ordained minister. One of her greatest accomplishments was to broker the union of the AWSA and the NWSA. The merger strengthened the presence of the suffrage movement.

That November, Elizabeth Cady Stanton turned eighty. The Metropolitan Opera House in New York City was "crowded pit to dome" with more than three thousand people there to honor her.[6] Stanton sat in a red chair on a flower-strewn stage and listened while Anthony read congratulatory messages. Stanton was in ill health, very fat and nearly blind, but still completely sharp in mind.

Susan B. Anthony spent the majority of the next year in California. Though she was seventy-six years old, she gave three speeches a day and helped direct a highly organized campaign. For the first time, wealthy women like Millicent Hearst, wife of the newspaper publisher William Randolph Hearst, gave money to the cause.[7]

Yet in the end the liquor lobby convinced enough men in California that women would pass laws banning alcohol if they were given the vote. Despite a long and valiant effort, the state amendment was defeated.

A LONG LIFE STORY

When she was in California, Anthony met a reporter from Indiana named Ida Husted Harper. Impressed with her skills, Susan asked the journalist if she might be interested in writing her biography. It will not be a lengthy project, Anthony assured her.[8]

Ida Harper went to Rochester expecting to stay a short while. Instead she found "boxes and bags of letters and other documents, dating back for a century."[9] Harper hired assistants to help organize the material while she interviewed Susan. For over a year, the group of women worked together closely in a bustling attic office. It was the longest stretch of time that Anthony had ever stayed at home since she was a girl.

That same year Elizabeth Cady Stanton had written her autobiography. She dedicated it to Susan B. Anthony, writing, "The current of our lives has run in the same channel so long it cannot be

Susan B. Anthony continued to work to support the suffragist cause, even in her later years. She could not rest or spend much time at home as long as women continued to be denied the right to vote.

separated, and my book is as much your story, as I doubt not, yours is mine."[10]

1898 marked the fiftieth anniversary of the first Women's Rights Convention in Seneca Falls. At the NAWSA convention that winter, Susan B. Anthony presided at the same round wooden table at which Elizabeth Cady Stanton had written the "Declaration of Sentiments." Behind her was a flag with four stars representing the states that had thus far given women the vote: Wyoming, Colorado, Utah, and Idaho.

In fifty years, much progress had been made. Much more was still required.

CHAPTER NINE

WORKING UNTIL THE END

The following summer Susan B. Anthony returned to London. The International Council of Women was meeting there and she had been asked to speak. Many different women's organizations were to be represented, with delegates arriving from Europe, North and South America, and Asia.

As one of the most important women's rights advocates in the world, Anthony was treated with reverence. Her speech was held at Westminster Hall in Parliament and the audience waved white handkerchiefs as a symbol of great respect.

Queen Victoria invited the conference leaders to tea. While a meeting with the queen would be an exciting event for most, Anthony was unimpressed, noting, "I cannot but remember that in all matters connected with women she has been very conservative."[1]

After the long sail home, Anthony went to stay with Elizabeth Cady Stanton at a mutual friend's vacation home in the Finger Lakes region of New York State. The women visited on a screened porch with views of the water. Anthony worried about Stanton's health, writing, "this infirmity having come upon her makes me fear that her time may be shorter than mine."[2]

Though she was still in very good health herself, Anthony was planning to resign as president of NAWSA. She was turning eighty and ready to pass the gavel. This did not mean she was ready to retire. As she told the convention delegates at the meetings in February 1900, she preferred to "see you all at work while I am alive, so I can scold you if you do not do it well."[3]

FANNIE LOU HAMER 1917–1977

As a poor African American woman living in racially segregated Mississippi, Fannie Lou Hamer was denied the basic rights of safety, education, and justice. When she first learned at forty-five years old that she was eligible to vote, her life changed completely. At great personal risk, she would end up voting, running for political office, and rising to national prominence as a civil rights activist. Following her example thousands of blacks registered to vote, finally participating in a system they had long believed was open only to whites.

On her birthday two weeks later, President William McKinley held a reception for her in the East Room of the White House. While the president had never openly supported suffrage, Anthony astutely made certain her visit was well publicized.

NAWSA held a big party in her honor. Frederick Douglass's grandson played the violin, and eighty children, one by one, presented her with a rose. Elizabeth Cady Stanton was too ill to attend but her daughter Hattie came and paid tribute in her place.

BIG SHOES TO FILL

Choosing her successor at NAWSA was a difficult task for Susan B. Anthony. Each of the young women in the corps known as "Susan's girls" was competent and dedicated to the cause of suffrage. Yet to Anthony two in particular stood out: Anna Howard Shaw and Carrie Chapman Catt.

Anna Howard Shaw was a woman of many accomplishments. Raised in impoverished circumstances in a log cabin in northern Michigan, she worked her way through college, divinity school, and medical school as one of the very few women in any of her classes.

Shaw became involved with the temperance and suffrage movements while tending to sick women in the slums of Boston. It was her talent as a speaker that first caught Susan B. Anthony's attention. Shaw traveled with Anthony to the campaigns in California and was closest personally to her among all the second generation women.

Carrie Chapman Catt grew up in Iowa where she attended college and became a teacher and journalist. After her husband died soon after their wedding, she turned to suffrage work. Known for her extreme discipline and strong organizational skills, Catt led the successful campaigns in Colorado and Idaho and labored hard in the tougher South Dakota, Kansas, and California.

Anthony chose Carrie Chapman Catt as her successor at NAWSA. Catt led the successful campaign for the Nineteenth Amendment. She also founded the influential League of Women Voters.

Because she believed that the suffrage movement in 1900 most urgently needed the know-how Carrie Chapman Catt would give it, Susan B. Anthony selected her over her close friend Anna Howard Shaw. Shaw stayed wholly involved with the cause and replaced Catt when she left office four years later.

Though Anthony had made her preference known, an official election was obligatory. When Catt's name was announced as NAWSA's new president, many of the convention delegates were emotional. One reported, "half the women were using their handkerchiefs on their eyes and the other half were waving them in the air. Mrs. Catt said quickly: 'Your president, if you please, but Miss Anthony's successor never! There is but one Miss Anthony, and she could not have a successor.'"[4]

NO LONGER FORBIDDEN GROUNDS

In September, Susan B. Anthony was distressed to learn that the plan for the University of Rochester to become coeducational was in jeopardy. Two years earlier she and Stanton had fixed terms which the university was now trying to renegotiate.

University trustees told Anthony that the agreement would be cancelled unless $2,000 was raised before a deadline the very next day. In order to keep the deal together, Susan pledged her life insurance.

The college agreed to admit women in its next class but the stress associated with the last-minute maneuvering caused Anthony to have a stroke. Her doctor ordered complete rest and for once in her life, Susan B. Anthony rested.

In mid-October she had recovered enough to go out for a short carriage ride. She asked to be taken to the campus. That night she wrote in her journal, "There are no longer forbidden grounds to the girls of our city."[5]

One hundred years after the birth of Susan B. Anthony, women in every state finally were afforded the vote. This photograph shows women lining up to vote in the 1920 election, shortly after ratification of the Nineteenth Amendment.

Almost exactly two years later Anthony received a telegram with news that while unsurprising, still brought her much grief. Elizabeth Cady Stanton had died. The funeral was planned for the next day at Stanton's apartment in New York City.

As Stanton had requested, the ceremony was private, nonreligious, and presided over by women. On her casket there were many flowers and a single framed photograph. The picture was of Susan B. Anthony, her partner in the great cause of her life.

For Anthony, Stanton's death was a great loss. In a letter to a friend she described the "awful hush — it seems impossible — that the voice is hushed — that I have loved to hear for fifty years."[6] Yet even without her closest ally by her side, Anthony responded in characteristic style. She went back to work.

THE NEVER-ENDING FIGHT FOR AN AMENDMENT

While Carrie Chapman Catt presided over the next NAWSA conventions, Susan B. Anthony remained its most influential spokesperson. In 1904 she testified before a congressional committee urging swift action on women's suffrage and demanding, "How long will this injustice, this outrage, continue?"[7]

On her eighty-fourth birthday at a reception in her honor at the White House, she approached President Theodore Roosevelt, who was then running for his second term. "Now Mr. President," she said, "we don't intend to trouble you during the campaign, but after you are elected, look out for us."[8]

That same year she went back to Europe. Rights advocates in Berlin had asked her to help them form an international suffrage association. Anna Howard Shaw traveled with Susan and saw first-hand the great respect she had earned abroad. Shaw told a colleague, "When the meeting was opened the first words of the presiding officer were, 'Where is Susan B. Anthony?'"[9]

Somehow Anthony kept up the same busy pace when she returned to the United States. At eighty-five years old, she boarded a cross-country train to Portland, Oregon, for the NAWSA convention. She had missed only one annual convention since the Civil War and saw no reason to miss another.

The next year the meetings were held closer to home, in Baltimore, Maryland. Anthony had a bad cold and the frailties of old age were finally weakening her. After the convention, she took the hour-long train to Washington, DC, where an eighty-sixth birthday celebration was planned.

Among many tributes read to her that evening was one from President Roosevelt who sent his congratulations but mentioned nothing about the suffrage cause. With her usual passion, Anthony replied that she wanted more than good wishes from the president. She wanted a constitutional amendment.

The adoring audience responded with cheers and tears. It was apparent to most in the hall that time was running out for their fiery leader. Anthony had one last message for them, declaring, "There have been others also just as true and devoted to the cause—I wish I could name every one—but with such women consecrating their lives, failure is impossible!"[10]

One month later, on March 13, 1906, Susan B. Anthony died at home with her sister Mary and Anna Howard Shaw by her side. Over the next two days, ten thousand mourners walked past her coffin draped with the four-star suffrage flag.

Her funeral took place in a blinding snowstorm. Wearing black graduation gowns and hats, female students from the University of Rochester served as pallbearers. Anna Howard Shaw presided over the ceremony and promised those assembled, "'Failure is impossible' shall be inscribed on our banner and on our hearts."[11]

CONCLUSION

It would take another fourteen years before Congress gave women the right to vote. On August 18, 1920, the Nineteenth Amendment granting women suffrage was ratified and became law. It stated, in part, "The right of citizens of the United States to vote shall not be denied or abridged by the United States or by any State on account of sex."

If Susan B. Anthony had been alive to see the battle won, she would have been absolutely joyous. For over fifty years, despite formidable resistance, she had challenged attitudes and laws that oppressed women.

She would have stopped for a day at most to celebrate. The next morning she would have gone back to work. A part of that attitude can be explained by her tremendous personal drive. By nature, she was unable to relax and her energy never flagged, even in old age.

Yet more to the point, Anthony would have been thrilled by another campaign just beginning. Getting the vote finally ushered women across the threshold to political life. New doors to opportunity opened at long last.

Make no mistake: Susan B. Anthony thought no right more important than the right to vote. While Elizabeth Cady Stanton made passionate arguments for women's freedom in marriage, Anthony single-mindedly sought the vote. She voiced many times over, "So long as women are a disenfranchised class the women can do nothing."

She led the effort to get the vote with a perfect balance of artful strategy and force of will. Susan B. Anthony was a truly gifted politician who charmed the press, lowly town officials, and U.S. presidents. At the same time she never once in her life eased off a grueling schedule of lectures, petitioning, meetings, and travel.

Because she was so disciplined, the suffrage movement itself was disciplined. Anthony made thousands of speeches and spent a staggering amount of time on the road. For forty years she was the prime mover behind the national conventions In Washington, DC, making certain that the cause remained a thorn in the side of Congress.

Susan B. Anthony's efforts to attain universal suffrage resonated long after her death. Her devotion to the cause of women is still felt today.

Because she was so pragmatic, she chose as her successor Carrie Chapman Catt, a virtuoso fund-raiser and organizer like herself, over Anna Howard Shaw, one of her closest friends.

Because she was so wise, she viewed women's suffrage as the critical first step to changing unequal laws and the beginning of a long journey. She understood that women had to have a voice in making the laws were they ever to achieve full citizenship and true equality.

On April 19, 2016, as New Yorkers headed to the polls to vote in the primaries for the presidential election, many women traveled to Susan B. Anthony's grave in Rochester to thank her for their right to vote.

Anthony's charisma engaged and mobilized the cause. She had a quirky sense of humor, a stubborn independence, and a resolute optimism. The younger generation of suffrage leaders owed an enormous amount to their affectionate but uncompromising mentor.

The nearly twenty-six million women who gained the vote in 1920 owed her their heartfelt thanks as well. Close to a century later, so do we all.

CHAPTER NOTES

INTRODUCTION. RESTRICTED

1. Jean H. Baker, *Sisters: The Lives of America's Suffragists* (New York: Farrar, Straus & Giroux, 2005), p.92.

CHAPTER 1. EARLY LIFE

1. Kathleen Barry, *Susan B. Anthony: A Biography* (New York: New York University Press, 1988), p.6.
2. Ibid., p. 19.
3. Geoffrey C. Ward, *Not For Ourselves Alone*: *The Story of Elizabeth Cady Stanton and Susan B. Anthony* (New York: Alfred A. Knopf, 1999), p.24.
4. Ida Husted Harper, *The Life and Work of Susan B. Anthony* (Indianapolis: Hollenbeck Press, 1891) vol 1, p. 29.
5. Barry, p.24.
6. Harper, p.38.

CHAPTER 2. THE STUDENT BECOMES THE TEACHER

1. Kathleen Barry, *Susan B. Anthony: A Biography* (New York: New York University Press, 1988), p.39.

2. Ibid., p.40.
3. *San Francisco Chronicle*, June 28, 1896.
4. Penny Coleman, *Elizabeth Cady Stanton and Susan B. Anthony: A Friendship that Changed the World* (New York: Henry Holt, 2011), p.44.
5. Geoffrey C. Ward, *Not For Ourselves Alone* (New York: Alfred A. Knopf, 1999), p.37.
6. Susan B. Anthony letter to her mother, *Susan B. Anthony Papers, Schlesinger Library of Radcliffe College*, October 15, 1848.
7. Ida Husted Harper, *The Life and Work of Susan B. Anthony* (Indianapolis: Hollenbeck Press,1898) vol.1, p.53.
8. Barry, p.52.
9. Lynn Sherr, *Failure Is Impossible: Susan B. Anthony In Her Own Words* (New York: Random House, 1995), p.xviii.
10. Eleanor Flexner and Ellen Fitzpatrick, *Century of Struggle: The Woman's Rights Movement in the United States* (Cambridge, MA: Harvard University Press, 1996), p.70.
11. Sherr, p.33.

CHAPTER 3. IMPORTANT PARTNERSHIPS

1. Jean H. Baker, *Sisters: The Lives of America's Suffragists* (New York: Farrar, Straus & Giroux, 2005), p.56.
2. Lynn Sherr, *Failure Is Impossible: Susan B. Anthony In Her Own Words* (New York: Random

House, 1995), p.189.

3. Elizabeth Cady Stanton, *Eighty Years and More: Reminiscences 1815-1897* (New York: Schocken Books, 1971), p.163.

4. Penny Coleman, *Elizabeth Cady Stanton and Susan B. Anthony: A Friendship that Changed the World* (New York: Henry Holt, 2011), p.9.

5. Ibid., p.61.

6. Kathleen Barry, *Susan B. Anthony: A Biography* (New York: New York University Press, 1988), p.72.

7. Sherr, pp. 135-136.

8. Ibid., pp.49-50.

9. Stanton, p. 51.

10. Stanton, p. 51.

11. Geoffrey C. Ward, *Not For Ourselves Alone*: *The Story of Elizabeth Cady Stanton and Susan B. Anthony* (New York: Alfred A. Knopf, 1999), p.80.

CHAPTER 4. WOMEN'S RIGHTS AND ABOLITIONISM

1. Lynn Sherr, *Failure Is Impossible: Susan B. Anthony In Her Own Words* (New York: Random House, 1995), p.4.

2. Ibid.

3. Ibid., p.32.

4. Kathleen Barry, *Susan B. Anthony: A Biography* (New York: New York University Press, 1988), p. 133.

5. Geoffrey C. Ward, *Not For Ourselves Alone: The Story of Elizabeth Cady Stanton and Susan B. Anthony* (New York: Alfred A. Knopf, 1999), p.95.
6. Ibid., p.100.
7. Sherr, p. 47.
8. Eleanor Flexner and Ellen Fitzpatrick, *Century of Struggle: The Woman's Rights Movement in the United States* (Cambridge, Massachusetts: Harvard University Press, 1975), p.105.
9. Jean H. Baker, *Sisters: The Lives of America's Suffragists* (New York: Farrar, Straus and Giroux, 2005), p. 72.

CHAPTER 5. A DIVISIVE BATTLE

1. Eleanor Flexner and Ellen Fitzpatrick, Century of Struggle: *The Woman's Rights Movement in the United States* (Cambridge, Massachusetts: Harvard University Press, 1975), p. 137.
2. Ellen DuBois, *Feminism and Suffrage: The Emergence of an Independent Women's Movement in America, 1848 - 1869* (Ithaca, NY: Cornell University Press, 1978), p. 54.
3. Flexner and Fitzpatrick, p. 140.
4. Kathleen Barry, *Susan B. Anthony: A Biography* (New York: New York University Press, 1988), p. 175.
5. Lynn Sherr, *Failure Is Impossible: Susan B. Anthony In Her Own Words* (New York: Random

House, 1995), p. 200.

6. Flexner and Fitzpatrick, pp. 144-145.

7. Sherr, p. 201.

8. Geoffrey C. Ward, *Not For Ourselves Alone: The Story of Elizabeth Cady Stanton and Susan B. Anthony* (New York: Alfred A. Knopf, 1999), p. 112.

9. Sherr, p. 81.

10. Ibid.

11. Jules Archer, *The Feminist Revolution: A Story of the Three Most Inspiring and Empowering Women in American History: Susan B. Anthony, Margaret Sanger, and Betty Friedan* (New York: Sky Pony Press, 2015), p. 51.

CHAPTER 6. A BOLD MOVE

1. Ida Husted Harper, *The Life and Work of Susan B. Anthony* (Indianapolis: Hollenbeck Press, 1898), vol. 1, p.387.

2. Lynn Sherr, *Failure Is Impossible: Susan B. Anthony In Her Own Words* (New York: Random House, 1995), p. 137.

3. Ibid., p.140.

4. Ibid., p. 215.

5. Penny Coleman, *Elizabeth Cady Stanton and Susan B. Anthony: A Friendship that Changed the World* (New York: Henry Holt, 2011), p.144.

6. Eleanor Flexner and Ellen Fitzpatrick, *Century of Struggle: The Woman's Movement in the United*

States (Cambridge, Massachusetts: Harvard University Press, 1975), p.159.

7. Douglas Linder, "The Trial of Susan B. Anthony for Illegal Voting", http://law2.umkc.edu/faculty/ projects/ftrials/anthony/sbahome.html (2001).
8. Ibid.
9. Ibid.
10. Geoffrey C. Ward, *Not For Ourselves Alone: The Story of Elizabeth Cady Stanton and Susan B. Anthony* (New York: Alfred A. Knopf, 1999), p. 148
11. Ibid.

CHAPTER 7. THE NEAREST EXAMPLE OF PERPETUAL MOTION

1. Penny Coleman, *Elizabeth Cady Stanton and Susan B. Anthony: The Friendship That Changed The World* (New York: Henry Holt, 2011), p.158.
2. Jean H. Baker, *Sisters: The Lives of America's Suffragists* (New York: Farrar, Strauss & Giroux, 2005), p.88.
3. Lynn Sherr, *Failure Is Impossible: Susan B. Anthony In Her Own Words* (New York: Random House, 1995), pp. 286-287.
4. Ibid., p. 240.
5. Ibid., p.166.
6. Kathleen Barry, *Susan B. Anthony: A Biography* (New York: New York University Press, 1988), p. 282.

CHAPTER 8. CHANGING A MINORITY INTO A MAJORITY

1. Penny Coleman, *Elizabeth Cady Stanton and Susan B. Anthony: A Friendship That Changed the World* (New York: Henry Holt, 2011), p. 182.
2. Geoffrey C. Ward, *Not For Ourselves Alone: The Story of Elizabeth Cady Stanton and Susan B. Anthony* (New York: Alfred A. Knopf, 1999), p. 186.
3. Lynn Sherr, *Failure Is Impossible: Susan B. Anthony In Her Own Words* (New York: Random House, 1995), p. 274.
4. Ida Husted Harper, *The Life and Work of Susan B. Anthony* (Indianapolis, IN: Hollenbeck Press, 1898), vol. 2, p. 753.
5. Ibid., pp.840-841.
6. Kathleen Barry, *Susan B. Anthony: A Biography* (New York: New York University Press, 1988), p. 308.
7. Eleanor Flexner and Ellen Fitzpatrick, *Century of Struggle: The Woman's Rights Movement in the United States* (Cambridge, MA: Harvard University Press, 1975), p. 216.
8. Harper, vol. 2, p. 909.
9. Ibid.
10. Coleman, p. 209

CHAPTER 9. WORKING UNTIL THE END

1. Kathleen Barry, *Susan B. Anthony: A Biography* (New York: New York University Press, 1988), p. 329.
2. Ibid., p.330.
3. Geoffrey C. Ward, *Not For Ourselves Alone: The Story of Elizabeth Cady Stanton and Susan B. Anthony* (New York: Alfred A. Knopf, 1999), p. 205.
4. Lynn Sherr, *Failure Is Impossible: Susan B. Anthony In Her Own Words* (New York: Random House, 1995), p. 321.
5. Barry, p. 335.
6. Sherr, p. 176.
7. Ida Husted Harper, The Life and Work of Susan B. Anthony (Indianapolis, IN: Hollenbeck Press, 1908) vol. 3, p. 1308.
8. Ibid., p. 1307.
9. Sherr, p. 309.
10. Ibid., p. 324.
11. Ibid., p. 326.

GLOSSARY

advocate — To speak or write in favor of something; someone who speaks or writes to support a cause.

agenda — A list or plan of things to be done, acted upon, or voted on.

canvass — To seek votes or opinions.

delegate — A person designated to act for or represent others at a political convention,

franchise — The right to vote.

gender — Either male or female as determined by social and cultural roles and behavior.

guardian — A person who is entrusted by law with the care of another person who is typically under the age of eighteen.

kangaroo court — A courtroom where customary law is disregarded, thus making a fair trial impossible.

lobby —To try and influence the votes of legislators.

petition — To ask for something formally; the paper itself on which the formal request is written.

radical — Favoring drastic or extreme political or social change.

ratify —To formally confirm or give approval to.

rhetoric —Exaggerated or pretentious writing or speech.

statute — An act made by a legislature and expressed in a formal document.

stipend — A fixed payment or allowance, typically of a lesser amount.

universal suffrage —The right to vote for any citizen, regardless of race or gender.

FURTHER READING

BOOKS

Archer, Jules. *The Feminist Revolution: A Story of the Three Most Inspiring and Empowering Women in American History: Susan B. Anthony, Margaret Sanger, and Betty Friedan.* New York, NY: Sky Pony Press, 2015.

Connors, Kathleen. *The Life of Susan B. Anthony.* New York, NY: Gareth Stevens Publishing, 2014.

Day, Meredith, and Colleen Adams. *A Primary Source Investigation of Women's Suffrage.* New York, NY: Rosen Publishing, 2016.

Edison, Erin. *Susan B. Anthony.* North Mankato, MN: Capstone Press, 2013.

Lusted, Marcia Amidon. *The Fight for Women's Suffrage.* Edina, MN: ABDO Publishing, 2012.

Nardo, Don. *The Split History of the Women's Suffrage Movement: A Perspectives Flip Book.* Mankato, MN: Compass Point Books, 2014.

Nash, Carol Rust. *Women Winning the Right to Vote in United States History.* Berkeley Heights, NJ: Enslow Publishers, 2015.

Penne, Barbra. *Susan B. Anthony: Pioneering Leader of the Women's Rights Movement.* New York, NY: Britannica Educational Publishing in association with Rosen Educational Services, 2016.

Wishinsky, Frieda. *Freedom Heroines: Susan B. Anthony, Elizabeth Cady Stanton, Jane Addams, Ida B. Wells, Alice Paul, Rosa Parks.* New York, NY: Scholastic, 2012.

WEBSITES

Susan B. Anthony: Celebrating 'A Heroic Life'
rbscp.lib.rochester.edu/susan-b-anthony
This website provides biographical information about Anthony, context about the women's suffrage movement, and a collection of photos.

The Susan B. Anthony Manuscript Collection
www.libraryweb.org/rochimag/SBA/intro.htm
This archive contains digitized manuscripts, letters, and ephemera written by Anthony and other suffragettes.

"Votes for Women, The Struggle for Women's Suffrage," Selected Images From the Collections of the Library of Congress
www.loc.gov/rr/print/list/076_vfw.html
This photo gallery contains hundreds of portraits of suffragettes, scenes from demonstrations and campaigns, and political cartoons.

INDEX